UNCOVERED:

THE LOST COINS OF EARLY AMERICA

T. Cook

The Lost Coins of Early Americans—Still A Secret!
by Todd Cook

Printed in the United States of America

ISBN 1-60034-429-1

www.xulonpress.com

To my darling little girl, Kaila LeAnne.

ACKNOWLEDGMENTS

I'd like to take this opportunity to thank a few folks whose efforts and support were crucial to producing this book. First off, I owe a huge debt of gratitude to my parents, Dean and Ruth Cook. Not only was their moral and financial support crucial to this work, but they were a huge help in the initial proofreading/editing of the early manuscript drafts. By the same token, a hearty thank you goes out LaVonne Ginn of Salinas, CA and Linda Sweet of Monterey, CA for their efforts in proofreading and editing the later drafts. I would also like to single out two of my former writing teachers, Nancy Brown of Quantico High School and Dr. Marcia Hurlow of Asbury College, who not only encouraged my early efforts, but inspired in me the notion that writing is a reward in itself. In the numismatic area, I'd like to recognize coin dealers such as Joel Anderson, Sal Falcone and Karl Stephens (among others), who not only have provided collector-friendly service to me over the years, but also provided a steady inventory of just the pieces described in this book. Lastly, thanks to everyone, family and friends alike, who offered their kind words of encouragement throughout the writing process.

UNCOVERED:
THE LOST COINS OF EARLY AMERICA

INTRODUCTION

In 1840, widow Dona Maria del Carmen Barreto decided it was time to move. She found life on her late husband's California estate bleak and lonely. Deep forests of pine, cypress, and oak trees dripping with Spanish moss cut off Dona Maria from the rest of California civilization. Though the ocean was nearby, it was a shoreline of sharp, jagged rocks and hostile, pounding surf. So Dona Maria sold her house and her land. With the $500 she received from the property, she bought a house in nearby Monterey. The 4,000 acres of wilderness land she unloaded for roughly 12 cents an acre is today known as Pebble Beach.

I know what you're thinking. Using Dona Maria's unfavorable real estate transaction as an opening anecdote, I'm going to proceed to point you towards FANTASTIC investment opportunities in rare coins! Opportunities to make the fortune that Dona Maria MIGHT have made, had she the foresight to realize the treasure she had in hand!

Wrong.

Yes, I'm excited about the coins we'll be discussing in this book, but I don't necessarily recommend them as "investments." At least not in the financial sense. True, if the word ever gets out on these coins and their fascinating connection to our nation's history, they COULD go up in monetary value. Then again, they may not. Most of the coins and tokens discussed in this book have barely moved up in price in the last twenty years! That's hardly the type of coin investment around which to plan your retirement. Later on in this book I will go into more detail as to why these coins and tokens MAY rise sharply in value, and also why they may not.

What I will say is this: by seeking out and obtaining the coins discussed in this book, you, personally, will be infinitely richer – you will be a caretaker of genuine treasures of our national heritage! You'll own what very few other Americans – rich, poor or otherwise – own: the very *first* coins that came over with and were used by the very first settlers of Florida, Virginia, New York and Massachusetts! You'll own the hard money that built the economy of this nation as it moved from an agrarian society to an industrial/economic power. Want to own an coin that was held by George Washington? It's absolutely possible.

And lest you think I'm the only one who believes such a collection is worthwhile, I'll do some name-dropping. John J. Ford Jr. is considered to be a "living legend" by expert coin collectors. Ford has built one of America's all-time great coin collections. Yet his advice to other collectors in a 2003 COINage magazine article is simple: " Buy scarce, important and overlooked coins and currency. " Ford goes on to marvel that, "You can buy a copper that actually was used in the latter part of the 18th century, before the Constitution was adopted.... You can buy that thing for $25! Why would you rather buy something that the Mint is making right now, coming out 70 or 80 or 200 a minute?"

The point is not to disparage the U.S. Mint or those who collect modern coins. The point is merely to say, if you're going to collect coins, why not consider TRULY scarce and historic coins in ADDITION to modern issues like the popular state quarters? Now I don't know what specific affordable 18th century copper coin Mr. Ford was referring to, but it could be one of a number of British, French, Spanish or American state-struck coppers that were floating around the streets of America in the 1700's. And when Ford says you can get an 18th century copper coin for $25, one that has connections to early America, I think he's actually quoting a high end price! But more than that, when it comes to building a coin collection, I'd like to focus on Ford's recommendation of "scarce, important, and overlooked" pieces, because to merit inclusion in this book, the pieces discussed must meet that criteria.

They must be SCARCE: The great thing about these coins is that they're all somewhat scarce. They have not survived to this day in the millions – or even the thousands in many cases! By comparison, even the "scarcest" state quarter has a mintage of around 200 million. The coins featured in this book are scarce enough that not everyone has one, or could even GET one (should every collector suddenly decide they wanted one). Scarce enough that you may have to do some hunting for them. Scarce enough that if there were ANY noticeable upswing in demand for these coins, supplies would dry up and prices would indeed skyrocket.

They must be IMPORTANT: These are the coins that came over with Christopher Columbus to the New World, coins that were held by the settlers of Roanoke Island's "Lost Colony" and Jamestown, coins that sailed the Spanish Main aboard pirate ships, treasure coins that went down in shipwrecks. These are coins that passed from hand to hand on "Wall Street" before Dutch Amsterdam became New York City! These are coins that circulated throughout the Thirteen Colonies in the years leading up to 1776! Need I go on?

They must be OVERLOOKED: Later in the book, I'll go into more detail as to just WHY these historical coins are overlooked by most coin collectors. For the most part, however, the reason can be summed up in one word: foreign. The coins and tokens discussed here are, for the most part, "foreign coins." Now the term "foreign coins," has largely fallen from favor as not terribly PC, so let's call them "world coins." Either way, these coins are passed over by most American collectors because they were NOT struck by the U.S. Mint. Most were not struck in this country at all, or even for use IN this country. So, most American collectors pass over these coins of England, Ireland, Spain, France, and Holland, in favor of U.S. coins struck from 1793 to the present. In doing so, many collectors of U.S. coins miss out on pieces that have a fascinating connection to our Colonial and early American past.

Yes, the coins discussed here are definitely scarce, important and overlooked. But many a scarce, important and overlooked coin still carries a price tag of $1,000 or more! That's even if you could track down a sample! And if you're anything like me, there's only so much enjoyment to be derived from reading about coins you'll never own. That's why, to merit inclusion in this book, the pieces must meet two more criteria: they must be AVAILABLE and AFFORDABLE! I know, I've already said these coins were "scarce." So how can a coin be both "scarce" and "available?" Well, they really ARE scarce – if you're trying to find them in antique shops or even your local coin shop. It may take some hunting, but you CAN find these coins. They are out there on the marketplace and ready to be purchased – if you know where to look!

And why are these old, historical coins so amazingly affordable – as in $50 and under, and in many cases, $25 and under? Simple! They're OVERLOOKED! (Remember reading that part?) Where there's limited demand, prices stay low. Until there is an upswing in demand, prices will remain low!

"Historical" is a term that is bandied about quite a bit when you see coins being hawked in big newspaper ads or on home shopping networks. Folks, the coins you're going to read about in this book are TRULY historical. They have million-dollar stories to tell. That they are scarce and important is understandable. That they are overlooked, available and affordable is unbelievable! But the fact that YOU can own these genuine historical treasures should excite you! I think it's worth plunking down the proverbial "$25" to own one of these coins. I hope, after reading this book, that you will agree with me.

CHAPTER ONE

"FIRST" COINS ARE
IMPORTANT!

"First impressions are the most important." Heard that one before? It especially holds true in coin collecting. Coin collectors love firsts! Casually mention to a Lincoln cent collector that you've come across a few 1909 Lincoln cents in an old cigar box, and watch his or her eyes light up! Why? Because even a novice collector of U.S. coins knows that 1909 was the first year the much-beloved Lincoln cent was struck! Of course, their eyes will also sparkle at the thought that one of those 1909 Lincoln cents might be a San Francisco issue with the initials "VDB" on the reverse, thus making it worth a few hundred dollars!

Let's think about another popularly collected U.S. coin: the silver dollar. Think any silver dollar collector worth their salt wouldn't want an example of our nation's first silver dollar? Of course they would! That's why collectors pay big money for any example of a U.S. Flowing Hair silver dollar of 1794–95. Obviously, any collector would prefer the first YEAR of that first silver dollar issue. But because the 1794 Flowing Hair dollar is so rare and costly, collectors of early silver dollars generally save up their money for the much more affordable 1795 Flowing Hair dollar. That way, they can at least say they have the first silver dollar TYPE struck by the U.S. Mint!

Going back even further into our nation's history are two other "first" coins that are highly coveted by today's collectors. Mention a "Fugio cent" to the layman on the street and you'll only get puzzled looks. Mention "Fugio cents" to knowledgeable coin collectors and right away they'll lecture you on how the 1787 Fugio cent was the first coin authorized by the authority of the United States, and is not only our nation's first large cent, but her first coin as well! That's why the bidding is lively when a Fugio cent comes up for auction, at a live auction or on eBay. Even more popular is the first official coin that rolled off the presses of our first United States Mint in Philadelphia: the 1793 Chain cent! The Chain cent has the distinction of being our nation's first large cent, first official one-cent coin (though Fugio cent collectors will argue with you on those counts), and our nation's first official U.S. Mint coin, period!

All this to say that America's "first" coins are usually pretty hot items. However, not every important "first" brings eye-popping prices on the coin market. The law of supply and demand still has to drive prices. If there are enough examples of even a popular and historically important coin to satisfy demand, prices will remain at affordable levels.

Case in point: the 1864 two-cent piece. It's a first-year-of-issue for this coin type. It's the first (and only) two-cent coin the U.S. ever struck AND is also the first U.S. coin to display the motto "In God We Trust." But all those factors, as of yet, have not translated into super high values for the 1864 two-cent coin: as of this printing, it's only about a $25 dollar coin in nice circulated condition. This is not an unpopular U.S. type coin, but there were millions struck, and enough survive today to fill the collector demand for this coin. In other words, while most collectors would agree that the

1864 two-cent piece is an important coin, and most collectors would certainly like to have one in their collection, that still doesn't mean large numbers of those same collectors are actively pursuing this coin. Not like they are the 1794-95 Flowing Hair dollar, or the 1793 Chain cent or the 1909-S VDB Lincoln cent!

In this book, you are going to learn about some pretty important "first" coins. In fact, some of the coins featured are strong contenders for the all-important title of "America's First Coin." And by my count, there are at least 16 contenders for that title– some are featured in this book, others may be mentioned, but are not featured. Why are there so many candidates? Because the definition of "America's First Coin" is somewhat flexible. For instance, by "America," do we mean the United States of America or all the Americas (as in North, Central, and South America)? Is our "first" coin the one that first plopped down on the soil somewhere in Canada by Vikings, or a coin that sailed over with Columbus? Does Colonial America begin in Spanish St. Augustine, Florida or British Jamestown, Virginia? Should America's First Coin be the first coin struck in America, or the first one SENT here to circulate? And on and on it goes– I think you get the picture. Happily, your definition can be just as good as the next guy's– provided you can back up your claim with at least some facts and coherent arguments.

Why should you be excited about owning one or more of America's first coins? Because they are the foundations of our nation's very earliest attempts at commerce! Forget about "alternative" Colonial mediums of exchange like wampum beads, tobacco leaves and gunpowder– the money we use today evolved from "hard-money" coins, not from a tobacco leaf! That makes these coins truly significant pieces of our heritage. In fact, in this book, no less than ten of the coins/tokens highlighted, are important "first" coins of our nation, in one sense or the other. And at least 8 of that 10 are, in my opinion, vastly overlooked by the collector market. Once again— and I will repeat this often throughout the book— these pieces are overlooked because coin collectors do not know about them yet! But you are about to. That's where you're going to have a tremendous advantage when you go out into the market to pursue these historical treasures!

In those chapters where an historical "first" coin is featured, a ribbon symbol will appear on the first page of that chapter. So take note. You'll want to go after these blue-ribbon winners. C'mon folks, how many people can say they own one of our nation's first ANYTHING? These coins may never win the prize of "most valuable." You probably won't be able to retire on what you'll receive from them should you ever decide to sell. But you won't regret owning them!

Because this book focuses (almost) exclusively on under-rated and neglected coins that can still be had for around $25 and under, some important "first" coins will NOT be spot-lighted, save for the brief honorable mention below. Pursue them if you can. The rest of us will simply cheer your good fortune:

1536-72 Mexico Silver 1 Real: Actually well within reach for most collectors as far as cost and availability. First struck in 1536, these coins are THE very first coins struck in the New World (Mexico City Mint). Highly recommended, but they are not under-rated. Consequently prices are rising at a steady pace for these. Currently it looks like you'll have to fork over at least $100 for an average circulated piece.

1652-87 Massachusetts Silver Coins: The first coins struck in Colonial America? The silver coinage of Massachusetts. These coins were struck IN the Massachusetts Bay Colony for use IN Massachusetts. The first of the Massachusetts silver coins were the crude and simple New England silver coins. But these coins with a simple "NE" on the face of them and the denomination marking (XII) on the reverse, are so rare and costly as to be virtually unobtainable. Much more obtainable and affordable are the later Massachusetts Willow and Pine Tree silver coins. But even these start around $1,000 even in low grades.

1688 American Plantation Token: A royally authorized token, struck by private contract as a base-metal (tin) coinage for Britain's American "Plantations," as the American Colonies were often referred. This is an American "first" coin in the sense that it is the first time the crown attempted to provide a coinage (of sorts) that would circulate throughout the Colonies. There is some controversy amongst numismatists today as to whether these Plantation Tokens, curiously given a Spanish-inspired value of 1/24 real each, ever circulated in America to any significant degree. Surviving specimens, even in low-grade, start at around $300.

1776 Continental Currency Dollars: Silver-dollar sized coins struck in silver, brass and pewter. Only the pewter pieces had anything close to a "sizeable" mintage, and that was only around 1,200 pieces. Many numismatists consider the Continental Currency coins to be an experimental, rather than a true coinage. But by the wear on some of them, it would appear some did reach circulation. It's very hard to find a genuine example, and when found, they too start at a couple of thousand dollars.

1787 Fugio Cents: Mentioned earlier. Prices continue to rise steadily on these, yet low grade examples can still be obtained for around $100 to $150. That's a big jump from just ten years ago, but the 'word is out' on these coins. They are highly sought after.

1792 Half Disme: A good many coin experts consider the 1792 half disme to be a pattern or experimental coinage. But as it appears that many of the estimated 1,500 half dismes did indeed circulate, just as many experts consider the 1792 half disme to be the first circulating coin of the United States, if not the U.S. Mint (which had not begun operations as of 1792). Even low grade examples, when they can be found, will run you at least $2,000– though that figure may double by 6 AM tomorrow morning.

1793 Chain Cent: Also mentioned previously. Our nation's first large cent. Our nation's first coin struck at the newly-established United States Mint. Struck only a few weeks in March of 1793, and discontinued because of the public outcry over the chain design on the reverse. Even lousy low-grade examples will cost around $1,500 while just passable average circulated pieces retail around $7,500!

That said, something interesting happened between finishing the first draft of this book and writing the final draft. I had to alter my theory as to which coin indeed wins the title of "America's First Coin." I believe I have recently found, if not a smoking gun, at least a very warm gun pointing to the piece that can truly be called "America's First Coin." At least by my definition. And my definition is this:

The first coin that came here in quantity for the purpose of circulating as coinage.

A chapter near the end of this book will discuss the smoking gun that, I believe, points to a clear cut "America's First Coin." And the great news is, that coin is one of the pieces spotlighted in this book. A coin that is definitely obtainable and still affordable!

CHAPTER TWO

A WORD ABOUT CONDITION

Before we delve in too deeply, we should pause a moment to discuss "condition." You can't talk about coin collecting without talking about condition. I wish you could, because debates over "condition" or "grade" often result in near-riots in coin collecting circles. Ok, that's a stretch, but not by much!

Why such contention over condition? Because real money is tied to a coin's condition. It's simple. If you purchase a coin that the dealer grades as "Very Fine," then he/she is going to charge you a "Very Fine" price. Imagine how unhappy you're going to be when you show your coin to another coin dealer or coin expert, and they inform you that the condition of your coin is no better than "Very Good," (which is two whole grades lower than Very Fine by the way). In other words, you paid the full $75 retail value for a coin that grades Very Fine when you should have only paid $10 for a specimen that grades Very Good.

Well, I'm not going to give you an in-depth study on all the official coin grades. I'm just going to explain what I mean in this book, when I refer to a coin or token as "low average circulated," "average circulated," or perhaps "pleasant circulated." Those are not scientific terms, but I feel they will do for the purposes of the coins discussed in this work.

When I quote prices, these would be prices one would pay for coins that have seen considerable circulation. These pieces will generally NOT have most of the original detail still intact. They will generally NOT be problem-free. I am taking into account that these old coins may have rim dings, worn spots, slight bends, some verdigris (fancy word for something that looks like moss), perhaps even a small not-too-unsightly hole.

Many of the coins I talk about are hammered coins. That means they were hand-struck, one-by-one, by means of hammer, tongs and probably a roaring fire just a few feet away. The strike, centering, shape of the coin, were only as good as the minter striking it that day! Hammered coins are seldom nicely round. They may not be fully struck-up; part of the design might never have gotten fully onto the face of the coin to begin with! These pieces may have flannel cracks. This is to say that such coins, generally struck before the mid-1600's, can be rather crude and not as uniformly sharp as later machine-made coins.

So, given the age of these centuries-old artifacts, as well as their sometimes crude method of manufacture, I will not be assigning strict numismatically-correct "grades" to go along with the prices. Besides, if you're going after coins such as these, I assume you're more interested in the history of these pieces than their strict investment potential — and investment potential is VERY strictly tied to condition or grade! We will not venture into that swamp here!

LOW AVERAGE CIRCULATED: By this, I mean a coin that may have only 50-75% of the original legend and design left. Intricate detail will be long gone. Still, it is easily identifiable, at least to the general type. The date may well be missing, but that would not be unusual for many 16th to 18th century coins. Dates were often struck very tiny and in low relief, not to mention nearly off the flannel! In strict numismatic terms, these might be your "About Good" coins, perhaps even the high end of "Fair."

AVERAGE CIRCULATED: These coins would also have seen considerable circulation, but the "basics" are pretty much intact. No real intricate detail will be left, except perhaps in small places here and there. The legend and date will be generally readable, though perhaps not sharp. In scientific coin terms, these might be your Good and Very Good grades.

PLEASANT CIRCULATED: Coins that have seen circulation, but are what I call, "no eye-strain-coins." Words in the legend/inscription, design and date are easily discernable without one having to strain their eyes! We even have some detail showing in the designs, such as hairlines on the head of the depicted ruler! Generally such coins would fall under the grade of Fine, perhaps even pushing Very Fine.

Most of the coins featured in this book, along with the prices quoted, will be for low to average circulated pieces. If you can find better and afford better, by all means go for the best condition you can afford! But if you're on a budget, don't feel ashamed of scooping up pieces in low to average circulated condition – especially not THESE pieces! The history is there no matter how they show their age!

1474-1504 Spanish billon blanca of
Ferdinand and Isabella

CHAPTER THREE

A COIN OF COLUMBUS AND 1492

(1454-74 Billon Blanca Of Spain)

Coinage in America began with Columbus. Yes, the Native Americans were here many centuries before the coming of Columbus and the European explorers/settlers, but the Native Americans didn't strike coins. So when Columbus came over in 1492, the Old World concept of coinage– not to mention coins themselves–came over as well. That's why, in my opinion, any collection of early American coins must start with a coin of Christopher Columbus. My pick for a coin of Christopher Columbus? A billon blanca of Spain, struck during the reign of Henry IV in the years 1454-74.

I can already see the question churning in your mind: "Why not start off with a Spanish coin struck during the reign of Spanish monarchs, Ferdinand and Isabella?" After all, it was Ferdinand and Isabella who sponsored Christopher Columbus' historic 1492 'Voyage Of Discovery' to the New World! We'll address that question later, but first, let's talk a little about that 1492 voyage of Columbus.

For all his documented faults and good intentions gone awry, Columbus dared to do what no one else at the time dared do. Columbus had the NERVE to try to convince to the highest powers of Portugal and Spain, that Asia could be reached by sailing (gulp) westward! Then, he set out to prove it.

Sailing out of the Mediterranean Sea and into the Atlantic Ocean doesn't seem very daring today, but it would if you were a European sailor in 1492. That's when the western ocean was known as the "Sea Of Darkness." Personally speaking, that name alone would be enough to keep ME from sailing out the Straits Of Gibraltar! Simply put, sailing westward beyond the horizon was next to madness. Even if you didn't subscribe to the popular notion that the western sea was filled with monsters, or that it ended in a gigantic drop-off into oblivion, there were other, more believable perils that awaited those who ventured out on the Sea Of Darkness. There were rumors of "mountains under the sea," that would rip apart any ship unfortunate enough to sail out that way. And if the mountains under the sea didn't get you, there were beds of seaweed so thick they could entrap ships and hold them fast as the boiling western sun baked all unfortunate souls aboard.

Most of us know the story in its basic form. In 1492, Columbus set sail with three tiny ships, the Nina, Pinta and Santa Maria, to find the westward passage to Asia. Most likely, at first, Columbus and his sailors were filled with optimism and bravado. But as they sailed far past the point where they thought land would be found, fear began to set in. It's one thing to set out for a known destination— it's quite another to set out for a destination that may not exist! No wonder there were loud cries for Columbus to turn back! No wonder there was a near mutiny. But you know the rest of the story. Land was at last sighted in October of 1492. When Columbus and his men set foot on that New World island, it was Columbus' most glorious moment. He had made history by doing what no man had ever done. He had crossed the western ocean and discovered Asia! At least that's what Columbus thought. Or DID he really think that? There are quite a few mysteries and/or controversies surrounding Columbus and his New World voyage. Let's look at a few .

MYSTERY #1: Exactly where did Columbus land? Historians all agree it was an island somewhere in the Bahamas. We do know Columbus named the island San Salvador, and indeed, there is an island in the Bahamas by that name. But many historians doubt that this island is the true landing site, especially since the CURRENT San Salvador island was so named in the early 20th century! There are about twelve islands in the Bahamas which can make a case for being the legitimate 1492 landing site.

MYSTERY #2: Did Columbus truly believe he had found Asia? Despite entering in his diary that he believed he had found the islands off the coast of Asia, many historians believe Columbus actually KNEW he had discovered a new continent altogether. Perhaps by referring to his discovery as merely "islands off the coast of Asia," he would discourage treasure-seeking settlers from crossing the ocean to exploit the wealth of this unsettled New World... which leads us to our third mystery.

MYSTERY #3: WHY is it so difficult to pinpoint the 1492 landing site? Shouldn't it be easy enough to follow Columbus' detailed voyage diary to verify which island was the true landing site? Ah, but here lie the problems: first, only about 20% of Columbus' diary are his own writings! The other 80% is a recount of his words as recorded by his son! Secondly, Columbus was somewhat vague in his recording of his historic voyage. In fact, in 1493, Ferdinand

and Isabella actually wrote Columbus, asking him for more precise details of the latitudes, longitudes, landmarks, etc., of the islands he had discovered! Again, historians believed Columbus wanted to stem the possible tide of fortune-seekers who would follow his trail to the wealth of the New World. There are more mysteries surrounding Columbus, but for us, the mystery is this: how can we get our hands on a genuine coin of Christopher Columbus?

THE COINS OF COLUMBUS: In the early 1990's, old coins were uncovered on an island in the Dominican Republic. REALLY old coins. Coins of the late medieval period! Even more interesting, these coins were excavated at the former site of La Isabel, the colony founded by Christopher Columbus in 1494, to which he made subsequent visits in 1496 and again in 1498. Scholars theorize that the coins were brought over in these later voyages.

The coins uncovered at the La Isabella site were mostly comprised of low denomination copper, billon (low-grade silver) and silver coins, dating from the late 1400's to the very early 1500's. The finds included copper coins of Portugal, a few copper and billon coins from Italy, and even one from Wurzburg, Germany. As you might expect, most of the coins were Spanish copper and billon coins. Of the nearly 80 coins excavated, it was the Spanish billon coins of Henry IV that turned up most often. By that standard, it's quite reasonable to make a case that these Spanish "blancas" of Henry IV are the leading candidates for the title of "First Coin Of The New World."

True, Spanish coins of Ferdinand and Isabella were also recovered at the La Isabella site. Wouldn't a coin of THESE monarchs better represent a true coin of Christopher Columbus? I have already mentioned their direct connection to Columbus and his 1492 voyage. Therefore I would say, by all MEANS go after a Spanish coin of Ferdinand and Isabella! They are incredibly historic coins and also quite available, as well as amazingly affordable– but also be aware that these coins are undated. Also remember that Ferdinand and Isabella coins were struck until roughly 1516, which means it will be very difficult (maybe impossible) to tell whether your Ferdinand and Isabella coin was struck circa 1492, or much later, perhaps into the 1500's.

You'll have no such worries with the coins of Henry IV. As they were struck no later than 1475, you can safely assume your Henry IV coin was circulating in 1492. It wouldn't even be too much of a stretch to surmise that a Henry IV coin or two sailed over to the New World on board the Nina, Pinta or Santa Maria! That's why my recommendation is a Spanish blanca of Henry IV. To hold one of these coins is not only to know it was around in 1492, but that a few came over to the New World in the mid to late 1490's as well!

Now for the really good news! Spanish billon coins of Henry IV are out there. It may take some searching, but they can be found. In fact, they regularly appear for sale on eBay and can also be found at larger coin shows. Look for dealers who sell older world coins. These charming old coins feature a crouched lion within a wavy border on the obverse, an ornate castle on the reverse. The design on each side is surrounded by a legend that is often hard to read. When you do find these coins, you'll find that they are not expensive, even in pleasant circulated condition! You might find a lower-end piece for $10-$15, a better circulated piece for $20-$35!

Folks, these are incredibly (I dare say, insanely) low prices for historical coins of this magnitude! You would do well to begin your voyage of early American coin discovery with these 15th-century Spanish classics!

c. 1516-42 Santo Domingo
4 Maravedis

CHAPTER FOUR

FIRST EUROPEAN COINS OF FIRST EUROPEAN SETTLEMENT IN U.S.?

(c. 1505-73 Santo Domingo Copper 4 & 8 Maravedis)

I believe there is a strong likelihood that, buried in the ground in a small plot of land off the coast of Georgia, there are at least a few crudely struck Spanish copper coins of the early 1500's. These would not be coins of Spain. These irregularly hammered coppers would have been struck in Spain, but the design would tell the bearer that this was a coin meant to circulate in the Spanish New World! If my hunch is correct, these roughly-made coins might well be the VERY first European coins to reach the soil of what is today, the United States. Certainly they would be the very first 'New World' coins to ever reach United States soil. These early 16th century copper coins may be broken into pieces or perhaps corroded beyond recognition. But I believe they are there. And I can even pin-point the year these coins were lost or left behind in the Georgian soil: 1526.

San Miguel de Gualdape. Ever heard of it? If you have, you're either from that tiny corner of the U.S. where the story took place, or you're a historian of the highest order. That there was a San Miguel de Gualdape on U.S. soil is a very VERY little-known fact. Yet, consider this: as of this writing, our country is just one year away from celebrating the 400th Anniversary of the founding of our first permanent British settlement, Jamestown.

Ah yes, Jamestown. The place where the United States of America was born. The very name conjures up images of Captain John Smith, Pocahontas, the first House Of Burgess in America, the capitol of Virginia from 1607-99, Bacon's Rebellion. Yet Jamestown very nearly passed into the same historical obscurity that now surrounds the name of San Miguel de Gualdape. The difference between the fates of San Miguel de Gualdape and Jamestown? A miraculously-timed arrival of a supply ship saved Jamestown from abandonment just two years after it was first settled. No such miracle saved San Miguel de Gualdape.

If you haven't guessed by now, San Miguel de Gualdape was the first European settlement on U.S. soil. Or DOES it deserve that distinction? After all, the tiny Spanish settlement didn't even last a full year before it was abandoned. There were other 16th century European settlements in what is today the United States that did not last. I have no problem conferring full "settlement" status on French Fort Caroline and British Fort Raleigh (both are discussed in other chapters), even though neither settlement lasted long. Yet I hesitate to confer full "settlement" status on San Miguel de Gualdape. To my thinking, the major difference is that outside forces conspired to obliterate Fort Caroline in 1564 and Fort Raleigh in 1587; the settlers of San Miguel de Gualdape simply couldn't make a go of it, so they left (not that I blame them, under the circumstances)! Still, you could argue quite favorably to give San Miguel de Gualdape its just due as the first European settlement on U.S. soil— it's certainly a valid argument. Nonetheless, the story of San

Miguel de Gualdape, and the coins possibly left behind at the site, is definitely worth telling.

Prior to 1525, Spain certainly knew of the region presently known as the southeastern coast of the United States. Spanish explorer Ponce de Leon had explored the balmy jungles of what is today Florida, in 1513. Ponce de Leon believed he would find the fabled "Fountain Of Youth" in the humid, thickly-forested region, but alas, such a fountain was nowhere to be found. Still, De Leon's 1513 exploration opened up an entire new region for Spain to explore and settle. It would take the passing of a few more years, but finally, around 1523, King Charles I of Spain sent conquistador Lucas Vazquez de Ayllon to explore the area of what is today the coast of South Carolina, and to find a water route to the Spice Islands in the Pacific Ocean. De Ayllon's explorations didn't uncover the hoped-for water route, but they did convince De Ayllon that the area was ripe for settlement.

Lucas Vazquez de Ayllon was not based in Spain. He has sailed west to the New World in 1502 to be a judge on Hispaniola, the island where the Spanish colony of Santo Domingo was located. De Ayllon was prominent enough in his position to mediate a dispute between explorer Herando Cortes and the governor. Then came the call from King Charles in the early 1520's to explore the Carolina coast, and, shortly thereafter, De Ayllon's decision to try and settle in this region of the Americas. So, in July of 1526, De Ayllon and six ships carrying some 600 settlers, set sail from the island of Hispaniola (today known as Haiti and the Dominican Republic) for the coast of what is today the Carolinas.

San Miguel de Gualdape would have been established on the South Carolina coast had it not been for one particular problem with the site: Indians. There were not enough of them! For those of us with preconceived notions of long-standing wariness and hostilities between Native Americans and European settlers, it seems highly improbable that 16th century Europeans would ever say to themselves, "We can't settle here, there are not enough Indians!" But that is indeed why De Ayllon and the settlers moved on from the Carolinas and headed south. Their reasoning was quite logical if you think about it. The Spanish knew they needed the help of the Indians to survive. The Indians knew how to cultivate the land for crops. They were skilled in the art of hunting local fish and game. The Spanish knew it would take time before they could farm and hunt well enough to provide for themselves. In the meantime, food would have to be procured by trading with the natives.

Finally, De Ayllon and the settlers found a suitable site, just off the coast of what is today Georgia. Nearby was a tribe of Guale Indians. San Miguel de Gualdape was established at this site. We can assume some kind of fort was built, but unfortunately, major problems began almost immediately. There arose a dispute over leadership between De Ayllon and some of the settlers. We don't know the exact nature of the disagreement, but we do know it resulted in another disastrous turn of events: racial warfare. And if you assumed it was warfare between the Spanish and the Indians, you'd be wrong. In another little twist that might not conform to today's popular notions, the straw that broke the camel's back of San Miguel de Gualdape was not Indian vs. Spanish conflict, but African vs. Spanish!

There was a slave revolt at San Miguel de Gualdape. You see, a number of African slaves were among the some 600 settlers who sailed to the Georgian coast from Hispaniola. Obviously, the slaves weren't happy being dragged to an even more remote region of the Americas to serve their Spanish masters. So when fighting over leadership broke out between De Ayllon and his Spanish subordinates, the slaves saw their opportunity for freedom. We know there was a slave revolt, though history doesn't record the extent of the bloodshed. We can only assume at least some of the Spanish settlers were slain during the revolt. The slaves then fled the settlement, and were said to have sought refuge with the local Indians. These Africans were the first blacks brought to United States soil to work as slaves. Their revolt was the first African-slave revolt on U.S. soil. Ironically, the San Miguel de Gualdape slaves fought for and won their freedom in the same land where countless other blacks, in the centuries that followed, found only slavery.

As for Lucas Vazquez de Ayllon, he survived the rebellion of his Spanish cohorts and the slave revolt. Then came the fever epidemic. De Ayllon and many of the other Spanish settlers died. This was the final fatal blow to San Miguel de Gualdape. The few remaining settlers who survived both the revolt and the fever epidemic abandoned the settlement and sailed back to Hispaniola. The eastern coast of the United States would not be settled again until the year 1564 (but not by the Spanish).

So how do coins play a role in this tale from history? Actually, I wouldn't say that coins played any great role, but anywhere there are coin-using people there are usually coins. San Miguel de Gualdape was a primitive settlement at best. It's doubtful a quantity of coins were brought to San Miguel for the purpose of circulation – as trinkets for trade with the Indians, perhaps. We do know the British brought copper coins and jettons to Fort Raleigh and Jamestown for just such a purpose. Other than that, I think it's safe to assume that the Spanish settlers of San Miguel were like settlers of other times and places: they sometimes brought a coin or two with them as a souvenir or 'lucky piece' from their homeland. In this case, that homeland (or at least the most recent one) was the island of Hispaniola. And fortunately for the coin enthusiast, there is one type of coin in particular that is directly traceable to Spanish Hispaniola of 1526: the Santo Domingo coppers of Carlos and Johanna.

The 16th century coppers of Santo Domingo are often touted as "First Coins Of The Americas!" Of course this can be quite confusing to the collector who sees the 1536-72 silver coins struck in Mexico City ALSO touted as "First Coins Of The Americas!" So which ARE the first coins of the Americas – the Santo Domingo coppers or the silver coins struck at Mexico City? Well, they both are. That doesn't make much sense to those of us who figure there can only be one winner in a foot race, but again it comes down to definition. Absolutely, the first coins STRUCK in the New World were the Spanish-Colonial silver coins struck in Mexico City beginning in 1536. The mint at Santo Domingo did not begin striking their copper coins (and ONLY copper coins) until 1542. BUT, the first coins struck for USE in the New World, were the copper 4 and 8 maravedis copper coins struck in Spain and sent to Santo Domingo to circulate. Moreover, these coppers were not just official Spanish coins that were exported to the New World, rather, they were struck specifically for New World use. So in THAT sense, the Santo Domingo coppers struck prior to 1536 are the "First Coins Of The Americas."

At this point, need you ask what kind of coins I believe are buried somewhere off the coast of Georgia? If there are coins buried beneath the ground of the San Miguel de Gualdape site, I believe they are Santo Domingo coppers. They would have been struck in Spain, packed into barrels and sent to Hispaniola on board a sailing ship. From there, they would have circulated in the colony of Santo Domingo for a time, then, brought up to present-day Georgia with a few of the San Miguel settlers in 1526. Shortly thereafter, during the commotion and suffering of the slave revolt and fever epidemic, the coins would have been lost or simply left behind at the site. Just what do these Santo Domingo coppers look like?

For starters, they're "round" in concept only. Since they were hammered into shape, one at a time, they come in all manner of "round" shapes. Some are rather thin, while others were struck on somewhat thick flannels. As for size, the 4 maravedis coppers are generally somewhat bigger than a U.S. quarter, while the scarcer 8 maravedis coppers are a little smaller than a U.S. half dollar. The obverse design features two crudely rendered crowned "Pillars Of Hercules," a design device often used on Spanish-Colonial silver coins from 1536 to 1772. On the reverse will be a 'Y' with two tails, though it also looks much like a big 'V.' The legend is often unreadable due to both wear, and uneven striking on the flannel.

The Santo Domingo coppers, by some accounts, were struck as early as 1505. Most experts, however, believe they were first struck around 1516. It's hard to say for sure, since these crudely struck copper coins are not dated. Those struck from at least 1516-56 were struck in the name of Spanish rulers Charles and Johanna. Their primary purpose for being struck, was to pay the Spanish soldiers (who were paid in the copper denomination of maravedis) charged with defending the colony of Hispaniola. When the Santo Domingo mint finally opened in 1542, there was such a copper shortage in the colony that the 4 and 8 maravedis coins were struck from melted–down copper bells and kitchen utensils. Consequently, the 16th century Santo Domingo coppers were often referred to as "Calderillas" or "little kettles." Also, the copper coins struck in Santo Domingo starting in 1542, have a mintmark of "S." Of course, any Santo Domingo coppers that might have made their way to San Miguel de Gualdape would have been those struck in Spain, sometime roughly between 1516-26. If you want a true coin of San Miguel de Gualdape, it would be a Santo Domingo copper of this period.

Still, in my opinion, ANY 16th century Santo Domingo copper is a worthwhile representative of San Miguel del

Gualdape. These old coppers were not dated, nor did the basic design ever change. Furthermore, these coins were seldom fully-struck up and most survive today in heavily worn condition. All this is to say that a Santo Domingo copper from the San Miguel de Gualdape period often cannot be distinguished from a Santo Domingo copper post-San Miguel de Gualdape. If you CAN pinpoint a Santo Domingo copper as at least a 1516-42 issue (pre-Santo Domingo mint) that would be the ideal "Coin of San Miguel de Gualdape."

Such early Spanish New World coins must cost a fortune today, right? Wrong again. I think there are two reasons for this. One, while the importance of the 16th century Santo Domingo coppers is well-known by world coin dealers, it doesn't appear that most collectors have the same under-standing of their importance. The information is out there, and certainly most eBay offerings of these coins talk up the "First Coins Of The Americas" aspect of the Santo Domingo coppers. But as of this writing, I just don't see a stampede by collectors to obtain these coins. It may well also be because a huge segment of the collecting community has it fixed in their minds that the 1536-72 Mexico City coins are America's "first" coins – which they are (in one sense).

Another factor that keeps the cost of these 1500's Santo Domingo coins down, is the supply. There are still enough on the market to keep prices VERY affordable. One source of the goodly supply of Santo Domingo coppers on the market today is a recently discovered hoard of these coppers found on the island of Jamaica. It is believed the hoard was buried when the Spanish Caribbean islands were attacked in 1586 by British privateer Sir Francis Drake. Still, it's mainly due to lack of collector demand that we DO have a supply of these old Santo Domingo coppers available today. Even with the Jamaican hoard, if as many collectors went after 16th century Santo Domingo coppers as have gone after scarce-date Lincoln cents, these early New World coins would vanish off the marketplace in a heartbeat!

So just how affordable are these historical coins as of this writing? $30-$40 seems to be the going price for an average (at best) circulated piece, and I would say the price most often lands in the $30-$35 range. I think it's still possible to get a just-identifiable, low circulated example for $15-$25. Keep in mind that even "high-grade" 16th century Santo Domingo coppers are extremely crude coins, some of the crudest coins ever rendered! The pre-1542 pieces, struck in Spain, would be the best-struck pieces, since the Santo Domingo mint pieces were largely hand-struck by unskilled (and probably quite unmotivated) Indian workers. You can usually find one or a few offered at any time on eBay (use search words "15* domingo" or "16th* domingo*"). If you should make it to a major coin show, search the offerings of dealers who sell Spanish and Spanish-Colonial coins. Some of the coins I discuss in this book are important but not essential. In my opinion, because of the combination of history, availability, and low-cost, the 16th century Santo Domingo coppers ARE essential for your collection of early American coins! Get one!

1565 England 6 Pence of
Elizabeth I

CHAPTER FIVE

FIRST COINS OF
THE BRITISH NEW WORLD

(1558-1602 Elizabethan Silver Coins)

We now jump ahead nearly 100 years to the mid-1500's. The mainland of what is now North America has been discovered; Spain has established a strong presence in what is today Mexico and South America; and while both Spain AND France have attempted to establish settlements in what is today the United States, Spain has succeeded while France has not– not yet anyway.

It is now 1587, and it's now England's turn to try their hand at settling the New World. In the summer of 1587, more than 100 settlers arrive at Roanoke Island, just off the coast of present-day North Carolina. A fort is established, but the men, women and children of Roanoke Island are fearful. The nearby Indian tribes seem to be growing more hostile, more threatening. Roanoke's Governor, John White, decides to return to England to try and bring back more fighting men. Before he leaves the island, however, he insists that the remaining settlers leave him some kind of sign as to their whereabouts should they be forced to flee the fort.

Upon John White's return to England, he finds his country preoccupied with the inevitable Spanish invasion. The invasion takes place, but Sir Francis Drake and his small fleet defeat the once "invincible" Spanish Armada. However, this doesn't do the settlers back on Roanoke Island much good, and it is another two years before Governor White finally gathers ships and reinforcements to return to the colony at Roanoke Island.

When White and his men finally arrive, they are dismayed to find that the colonists have disappeared! The fort is in ruins, completely abandoned, but, carved onto a fort post is the word, "Croatoan." From this, Governor White and his men assume that the colonists have fled to nearby Croatoan Island, where the native inhabitants were known to be kinder than the other nearby native tribes.

White and his men sail on to Croatoan Island, but there they find no trace of the colonists nor of Indians. A storm is now bearing down on their ship, and it's too risky to continue the search. White and his party abandon the search, assuming the colonists are all dead. To this day, the settlement at Roanoke Island is known as the "Lost Colony." It will also go down in history as Britain's first New World settlement. It will not, however, be until 1607 that the first *permanent* British New World settlement is established. That would be Jamestown in Virginia.

Now, let's talk coins. What do we know of the coins, if any, that came over to Roanoke Island's "Lost Colony?" Well, apparently some coins did come over. Around 1703, an English traveler named John Lawson wrote that various artifacts had been found at the Roanoke Island site, among them, " some old English coins." Lawson did not specify what those "old English coins" were, but a later documented find gives us a good idea.

In his book, <u>The Virginia Adventure</u>, noted Colonial archaeologist and author Ivor Noel

Hume writes:

> *It is a pity that Lawson did not identify the coins (though he may not have seen them), for none has been found on the site. But on private property not far from it an Elizabethan silver sixpence of 1563 has been unearthed from the roots of a tree. Carefully pierced for suspension, apparently by means of a steel drill, the coin was almost certainly given to the Indians by the English as a portrait of the Indians' new queen. As such, it is both the earliest surviving example of such a gift and the earliest known portrayal of Queen Elizabeth to be seen in America.*

And that's not all. Elizabethan silver coins of varying denominations have turned up in excavations at the Jamestown Fort site as well! In other words, folks, if you're looking for the first coin of the British New World, look no further. If you hold a hammered British silver coin struck during the reign of Elizabeth I, you are holding a coin that the settlers of the "Lost Colony" and Jamestown would have carried with them as they struggled to gain a foothold in the New World!

Does that mean that Elizabethan silver coins are our first Colonial coins? In my opinion, they are coins that did indeed come over to America, but I don't believe they can be considered "Colonial coins." In other words, I don't believe Elizabethan silver coins came over as coins that were intended to circulate. I believe they came over as souvenirs, as keepsakes from the Mother Land. They were probably brought to be used as gifts for the Indians. There is no evidence of a hoard of Elizabethan silver coins being found on a Colonial site. Such a find might indicate a supply was sent over from England to circulate in the Colonies. Neither is there any documented evidence to that effect.

But come over they did, and your collection of America's earliest coins absolutely must include an Elizabethan silver coin! Your greatest challenge will be finding a piece with a decent portrait of Elizabeth. Typically, the queen's bust was struck in low relief compared with the rest of the coin, and is often found completely worn off! In fact, be prepared for a big price jump for an Elizabethan coin with a strong, detailed portrait of Elizabeth. However, if you're willing to settle for a coin of lesser quality (chipped rim, small hole, worn portrait), you can obtain a history-filled Elizabethan coin for $15-$35! A just-identifiable coin can run even lower!

There are various denominations of Elizabethan silver coins, from the tiny silver penny to the large-sized shilling. Because it's been documented that Elizabethan sixpences have turned up both at Roanoke Island and at the Jamestown site, the sixpence is my top choice for the Elizabethan coin that belongs in your collection. The smaller groat and the large shilling would also be worthy inclusions.

Elizabethan coins are no secret to coin collectors– at least those who collect older world coins. The coins of Elizabeth I are quite popular and sought after– but more so for their BRITISH history! Elizabethan coins conjure up images of Britain's Golden Age: of William Shakespeare and plays at the Globe Theater; of the defeat of the Spanish Armada in 1588; of daring sea voyages by Sir Francis Drake, and, of course, of the legendary "Virgin Queen" herself, who ruled with a strong hand for nearly fifty years!

Elizabethan coins are full of fascinating history, both British AND American! But until the hoards of American collectors catch on that these coins are a huge "first" in our nation's monetary history, prices for these coins will remain reasonable. Go out and find one before prices go higher!

1550-1620 Brass Jetton of
Nuremberg, Germany

CHAPTER SIX

GAMBLING MONEY
OF THE "LOST COLONY"
AND JAMESTOWN

(1550-1660 Brass Jettons Of Nuremberg)

Elizabethan silver coins were not the only "coins" found at the excavated sites of Fort Raleigh and Jamestown. Also found at both historic sites were these pieces: brass jettons struck in Nuremberg, Germany.

A jetton is not actually a coin. A jetton is not even a token. But it looks just like a coin, and is often mistaken for a coin. Like most coins of Western manufacture, jettons are round, they have legends that encircle a design on the obverse and reverse, and some even have dates. What jettons do NOT have is a stated monetary value.

Just what are jettons? Jettons were first struck in the Middle Ages. Their original purpose was to serve as counting aids for merchants, much like the round wooden beads on an abacus. By the time the 1500's rolled around, jettons began to have another popular use – as a kind of gambling money. You might say they were a forerunner of today's gambling chips. Even so, while jettons are not coins, they are numismatic items – close "kin" to coins and tokens, if you will.

Jettons were struck in England, France, Germany and the Netherlands. By the mid-1500's, however, the chief manufacturers of jettons in Europe were undoubtedly the jetton-makers of Nuremberg, Germany. Though from the 1540's through the 1660's the Nuremberg jetton designs varied, the most common design was this: a three-crowned fleur-de-lis surrounded by a legend on the obverse; on the reverse, a cross and orb surrounded by a legend. These Nuremberg jettons or counters, were highly popular in Tudor and Stuart era Britain! In fact, it is still pretty common for them to show up in England metal detector finds!

Given their popularity in 16th and 17th century England, it shouldn't be surprising that these jettons would show up at our earliest British Colonial sites. Archaeologist Ivor Noel Hume notes in his book, The Virginia Adventure, that three Nuremberg jettons had been found at the Roanoke Island "Lost Colony" site, and copper "coins" found by 17th and 18th century visitors to the ruins were likely Nuremberg jettons.

Hume further writes:

Made by Hans Schultes of Nuremberg, who was working between 1550 and 1574, the jettons are the most closely datable artifacts from the site. But they do more than that. Thanks to them, there is convincing evidence of a connection between the Roanoke fort and an Indian site forty miles away at Buxton near Cape Hatteras, where in 1938 an identical jetton was found. The Buxton site had been home to Indians of the Croatoan tribe, a name wri large in the final act of the Roanoke drama.

Apparently a goodly number of Nuremberg jettons reached the early Virginia settlements as well. William Kelso, Director of Archaeology for the Jamestown Rediscovery I project writes:

The numbers of objects dating to the 16th century or predating 1607 are surprising. These include seven jettons, or casting counters, which are coin-like objects that originated in the Middle Ages as mathematical aids in the casting of accounts.. However, jettons became calculating tools for games by the Jamestown period. While casting counters typically appear on early 17th century sites in Virginia, they are usually types made by Hans Krauwinckel II of Nuremberg in the period 1580-1620.

Even further proof of the Nuremberg jetton's important connection to early Colonial history is the 1580-1620 Nuremberg counter that turned up in the vicinity of Martin's Hundred, a small plantation settlement located near Jamestown. Martin's Hundred was largely wiped out in a 1622 Indian attack. Martin's Hundred will discussed later in this book as well.

What purpose would a Nuremberg jetton have served to a settler in the New World? As mentioned in the above passage, they were likely used by colonists and soldiers as a kind of gambling money. Games of chance were handy ways to pass the long evening hours after the day's work was done. It is also theorized that jettons were brought to America to be used in trade with the Indians. The 1550-74 type jetton found on Roanoke Island would seem to hint at this. That piece was holed and likely strung to be worn around the neck of a local native.

Are these humble yet historic brass pieces still available to the average collector? Absolutely! Dealers who sell older world coins and tokens might well have them in stock. What these dealers usually DON'T have, however, is the historical background to which YOU are now privy! As a result, these early Colonial-related artifacts often go begging on the market! As of this writing, these jettons seem to run about $8-$12 for an average specimen. A low grade piece might go for $5 or less! There is no real standard guide for 1550-1660 Nuremberg jettons, so prices can be all over the board. Rarely do I see one priced at over $20 unless in very high grade.

If you're searching for a piece on eBay, simply type in the search words, "jetton" or "jeton" (the spelling seems to be evenly divided between one 't' or two) or "counter." Also, if you're searching under the 'Coins' category, they can also show up when you type in the search words, "hammered" or "medieval" (they are often mistaken for medieval coins).

Is there any way to date these Nuremberg jettons? I have encountered only one dated piece, a 1553 Nuremberg jetton. Generally, though, these jettons do not bear dates. A good rule of thumb to follow is this: if you see the name 'SCHULTES' in the legend, then your jetton dates roughly 1550-74. If you see the name KRAUWINCKLE' in the legend, your piece dates about 1580-1620. These 1580-1620 jettons would be the most common types found in Colonial America. So while you may never dig up one of these historical jettons from the sands of Virginia or North Carolina, you may very well dig up one in a dealer's loose coin tray!

1601-02 Ireland Copper Halfpenny Token

CHAPTER SEVEN

COINS OF THE 1607-10 JAMESTOWN FORT!

(1601-02 Irish Copper Halfpence & Penny Tokens)

O f all the pieces we'll be discussing, these copper tokens are probably the most obscure. They were struck for only two years: 1601 and 1602. They were struck in England during the last years of Queen Elizabeth I's life. These copper tokens were struck in halfpence and penny denominations. But they were produced to circulate in Ireland, not in England. The citizens of England would turn their nose up at a copper "penny," especially considering they already had a silver penny AND silver halfpence. The Irish weren't thrilled either with this base-metal token coinage struck for them by the British crown – but let's not delve into that history. Suffice it to say, this largely inconsequential copper should receive its due as a coin of our first permanent settlement, Jamestown.

That is not to say that these 1601-02 Irish tokens were the only "coins" to come over to Virginia with the first Jamestown settlers. Excavations at the early fort site show that Elizabethan silver coins came over also, as did a few small-denomination silver coins of James I. But unlike the silver coins of Elizabeth I and James I, the 1601-02 Irish tokens seem more likely to have come over by design, not by happenstance, or because one of the settlers wanted a souvenir from back home. More on these historic halfpence and penny tokens later. Right now, you may be reading this and thinking to yourself, "Jamestown, Jamestown – what's so important about Jamestown?" Well, if you weren't paying attention in history class, I'll try and give you a brief review.

The United States of America began at Jamestown. That's true even though the Spanish and French were here years before. That's true even though the first British settlement in America was at Roanoke Island in present-day North Carolina, but that settlement didn't last. Jamestown did. Though to some that's stating the obvious, I get the impression that today, more Americans are familiar with "Pilgrims" and "Plymouth Rock," than they are with Jamestown. That's why I feel it's important that every American should have some knowledge about this small but immensely important 17th century settlement, located along the James River in southeastern Virginia. So now, on with the story.

In December of 1606, three ships set sail from England carrying onboard 144 men. Average age: 27. Though there were some soldiers and craftsmen among that number, many of the 144 were "gentlemen," a segment of English society woefully inexperienced in the art of manual labor and wilderness survival. Their intent: to establish a settlement that would extend Great Britain's empire into the resource-rich New World. More specifically, this band of settlers was out to enrich their sponsor, the Virginia Company of London with treasures from the New World (i.e gold and silver) and at the same time grow their own fortunes. It didn't quite work out that way.

The three ships crossed the Atlantic and landed at what is today the coast of Virginia. The ships then sailed up the James River inlet, looking for a suitable sheltered spot where hostile Spanish ships could not get to them easily. The ships eventually landed at their chosen site in May of 1607, and immediately set about building the Jamestown Fort. Almost at once the search for gold and silver got underway, but the men found only water and wilderness. On top of that, disease, famine, death and shaky relations with the local Algonquin Indians discouraged the new settlers of Jamestown. The settlement was nearly abandoned, but a supply ship arrived just in time to persuade the departing settlers – who were in the process of sailing down the James River towards the Atlantic — to return to Jamestown.

But it was not just the newly arrived supply ship that helped save Jamestown. Jamestown survived in no small part because of the efforts of Captain John Smith. Smith was not exactly Mr. Popularity in the Virginia colony – he seems to have been rather loud, bossy, obnoxious, impulsive, and boastful. Most historians tend to believe he stretched the truth in his tale of how Pocahontas, daughter of the great chief Powhatan, stepped in to save him from execution at the hands of her father's warriors. Still, it was Smith who whipped into shape the band of Jamestown gentleman settlers, insisting that those who would not work would not eat. It was Smith who led scouting expeditions throughout the surrounding area, formulating a plan to defend against and at the same time, work with the local Indians to ensure the colony's survival.

Despite numerous hardships, Jamestown did survive. The House Of Burgesses was formed here in 1619, thus ushering in our first representative government in America.

The settlers quickly learned how to plant their own crops and become self-sufficient. A neatly laid-out town grew up just outside the walls of the fort; thus, the James Fort became Jamestown. In 1622 Jamestown survived a widespread Indian attack that devastated outlying settlements – Jamestown was able to prepare for and stave off the attack thanks to a warning from an Indian boy. In 1676 Jamestown was again threatened with violent destruction, this time from a citizen-led rebellion led by a man named Nathaniel Bacon. Bacon and his followers marched on the home of Governor White who stood up to Bacon and the rebels. Violence was averted.

Finally, when fire destroyed the statehouse in 1698, it was decided that the capital of Virginia should be moved from Jamestown to a more suitable, higher-ground location. So, in 1699, the capital site was moved a few miles away, to the tiny burgh of Middle Plantation. There, a city plan was mapped out, and Middle Plantation's name was changed to Williamsburg, in honor of the reigning British monarch, King William III. As the "action" was now in Williamsburg, Jamestown declined into a quiet, sleepy, riverside village. By the dawning of the 1800's, Jamestown could just as well have renamed itself, Ghost Town.

As the history of our nation marched on, Jamestown eventually disappeared above-ground, save for the old c. 1640's brick church tower. By the 20th century, it was believed that the Jamestown shoreline had eroded to the extent that the original James Fort site was all underwater. In the 1990's, excavations near the old church site revealed that the location of the original 1607-10 fort was not underwater after all! It was still on the Jamestown Historic Site Park grounds, just feet away from the early 20th century seawall! That's when excavations brought to light numerous 1607-10 James Fort artifacts, including coins! And folks,

TWENTY-FIVE of the coins found were 1601-02 Irish copper tokens!

Were these 25 (and there were likely more) small Irish tokens sent to Virginia to circulate as Colonial money? It would appear so, but it's not certain. Some historians speculate that the Elizabeth I Irish copper tokens served a two-fold purpose: as a circulating medium for small transactions between colonists, and as trade items with the Indians (who absolutely loved copper items). Then again, there's also the possibility that these Irish tokens were simply the private stash of an Irish soldier, or a British soldier who had fought in the recent wars in Ireland. At this writing, there is no evidence that these Elizabethan Irish tokens found their way to any other early American settlements outside the 1607-10 James Fort.

The designs are simple: on the obverse is a crowned harp, with the date divided on both sides of the harp. On the reverse, a shield of arms subdivided by a thin cross. You would see "ELIZ" in the legend, if the legend is intact. When seeking out one of these 1601-02 Irish tokens, don't worry about denomination. It doesn't matter whether you procure a halfpenny token (about the size of a U.S. cent) or a penny token (slightly larger than U.S. cent). Both denominations came over to Jamestown, neither one being more important than the other. The trick is finding one of these fairly scarce tokens at all. In fact, of all the coins and tokens featured in this book, the 1601-02 Irish tokens may be the hardest to find.

That doesn't mean these tokens should retail for super high prices. In fact, the 2005 edition of Krause Publications' Standard Catalog of World Coins 1601-1700 shows values of only around $15 for an average circulated piece, halfpenny or penny. Still, I've noticed that when one of these tokens DO show up on eBay – and usually I see no more than two or three listed in any given week, some weeks none at all– they bring in pretty strong prices. I would expect to pay $30-$45 for an average circulated piece, perhaps $20-$30 for a low circulated piece. Recently, I was fortunate win a low circulated halfpenny token (dateless) on eBay for around $9. I was able to obtain a couple more, in absolutely horrendous condition, as part of a three-token offering from Ireland. The cost: $11.

If you are looking for one of these tokens on eBay, try typing in the search words, "160* Irish" or "160* Ireland." Those search words should be enough to ferret out any 1601 or 1602 Irish copper token up for auction. The identified ones, that is. If you happen across any grouping of hammered coins being sold from an Ireland location (search words: "hammered coin*") look carefully to see if you can spot one of these historic coppers.

As a final note, I visited the Jamestown and James Fort site shortly before writing this chapter. It was in mid-April. The day was sunny but chilly winds were blowing in off the James River. The ocean was not far away and, no doubt, the cold Atlantic Ocean air was blowing up and across the massive James River. I stood on the flat grassy shore where America's first permanent settlement once stood and looked down at the rough, swift current of the James River, seemingly just INCHES below where I stood! Minutes before, I had crossed over a foreboding swamp to the Jamestown site on a modern walk-bridge. This was the same infamous swamp I'd read about in grade school history class; the swamp that caused so much death and disease in the early years of the Jamestown settlement. "What a terrible place for a camp-out," was the thought that kept coming to my mind. Today, it's a fascinating historical site, yet what a place of sadness, hardship and discouragement for the British settlers who struggled to gain a foothold here in 1607.

Perhaps by tracking down a 1601-02 Irish token, you too can feel a connection with the (mostly) young British men who never dreamed that their unpromising venture in the wilds of Virginia, would eventually blossom into something called The United States of America, a great and powerful nation that would stretch from sea to shining sea!

1614-25 England Patent Farthing of James I

CHAPTER EIGHT

OUR NATION'S FIRST
WIDESPREAD COLONIAL COIN?

(1613-25 British Patent Farthing Of James I)

You'll remember that when we were discussing the 1601-02 Irish tokens found at Jamestown, I stopped short of declaring these tokens as our "First Colonial Coin." A candidate? Definitely. Well this chapter deals with ANOTHER candidate for the title of "First Colonial Coin." The 1613-25 British Harp Farthings of James I. These are also known as "patent" farthings, as they were struck not by the crown, but under patent FROM the royal crown.

Have these farthings been excavated in great number at early Colonial sites? Actually, no. In fact, I don't know that we've found as many of these farthings as we have the twenty-five Elizabethan Irish tokens! Hmm, all right. Then perhaps we're talking about them because the James I farthings were struck for the specific purpose of circulating in the Colonies. Well, no. They were meant to circulate in Great Britain. "Well then," you ask, "why should these James I farthings be considered the first Colonial coin of British America?" I'll get to that, but first a little background on their Colonial connection.

In 1980, an archaeologist named Ivor Noel Hume was excavating the site known as Martin's Hundred. Martin's Hundred and its main village of Wolstenholme Town, was located about ten miles east of Jamestown in Virginia. Martin's Hundred was meant to be a plantation-type society. First settled in 1618 or 1619, disaster struck the tiny British settlement in the form of a devastating 1622 Indian attack. Out of some 140 settlers, 78 were slain. Only a warning from an Indian boy saved nearby Jamestown, as that warning provided the settlement the opportunity to prepare arms and defend itself. A few of the surviving Martin's Hundred settlers returned to the plantation, but it never fully recovered. By the mid-1600's, Martin's Hundred was pretty much abandoned, not to see the light of day again until Mr. Ivor Noel Hume and his crew began excavations in the late 1970's.

Among the coin and coin-related artifacts uncovered were these: a small silver Spanish coin, a 1580-1620 Nuremberg jetton, and two British patent farthings of James I. It was these two James I farthings that Mr. Noel Hume found particularly telling. The first farthing in particular. The first of the James I farthings found had a tin coating still intact. Most interesting. Why? Because tin-coated James I farthings were only struck for three months in 1613. This very first tin-coated issue of the James I farthings proved to be highly unpopular in Great Britain, for it was extremely tiny in size and weight. Furthermore, the tin coating was quite thin and tended to wear off quickly. I suppose the tin-coating was to make the farthing more acceptable to the populace, the hint being that the farthings contained a smattering of silver. Being unpopular, the tin-coated 1613 farthings were replaced by a slightly larger issue (now classified as Type II). These were not all that popular either. Type I and Type II James I farthings are today also both classified as "Harrington Farthings." The THIRD issue of 1614-25 (generally known as Lennox type farthings) proved to be somewhat more acceptable.

But though James I farthings are broken down into sub-type (I, II and III) and contractor type (Harrington and Lennox) classifications, the basic design never changed. The obverse featured crown and scepters, surrounded by a legend. The reverse featured a crowned harp surrounded by a legend. In the obverse legend "JACO" identifies the farthing as a James I issue ("JACO" being the abbreviation of the Latin name for James, "JACOBVS").

But back to the tin-coated farthing found by Mr. Noel Hume. Why, he wondered, would a virtually uncirculated farthing struck for only three months in 1613, turn up in the Virginia wilderness some five or six years later? If this 1613 farthing had circulated for any length of time, the tin coating would certainly have worn off.

Later in the excavations, another coin turned up, a 1613-14 patent farthing of James I. Now the official count was two out of three coins (not counting the jetton) found at the Martin's Hundred site being 1613-14 James I farthings. With this in mind, Ivor Noel Hume put forth this theory: the unpopular early issues of James I farthings were recalled throughout Great Britain, stored, then five years later exported to the Virginia Colonies where they would find more acceptance.

But that's not the last glimpse of these patent farthings in the Virginia Colonies. In 1636, the Governor of Virginia petitioned King Charles I for a fresh supply of farthings to be sent to Virginia. Apparently they were well-liked in Virginia up until that time. That petition (no evidence that it was granted by the way) indicates a usage in the Virginia Colonies from at least 1618 through 1636!

We also know that the British patent farthings must have been familiar to the colonists up in the Massachusetts Bay

Colony as well. Why? Because they were NOT popular up there. In fact, legislation was passed in 1635 stating that the British farthing tokens would no longer pass for a farthing in Massachusetts, rather a "lead musket ball" would pass for the value of a farthing!

What does all this tell us? It tells us that the British patent farthings found their way to the Virginia Colonies as early as 1618. They were familiar not only to the Virginia colonist (yes, a few have been found at the Jamestown site as well) for a full generation, but to the Massachusetts colonists as well! These farthings were low enough in value and unpopular enough in the Mother Country to warrant being exported to the New World for the specific PURPOSE of being circulated here. It all adds up to this: these farthings are quite arguably British America's first widespread Colonial coin! Is this theory widely accepted amongst top numismatists? Not yet anyway. But I believe Ivor Noel Hume makes an excellent case!

Notice, I've taken the American history of these farthings at least into the 1630's. After 1625, however, the James I harp farthings became the Charles I harp farthings – the same design, roughly the same size, different king's name in the legend: now instead of "JACO" there was "CARO," short for "CAROLVS," Latin name for "Charles." Then, in 1634 the harp design on the reverse changed to a crowned rose. The Charles I rose-design farthings were struck until 1645. After that, the tiny copper patent farthings passed into history. The British farthing would reappear in 1672, but this time as a larger, sturdier coin struck not by private patent, but by the crown itself!

Ideally, the farthing you should seek for your collection would be a James I type. Of course, the scarcer 1613-14 James I farthings have the stronger Martin's Hundred/Jamestown connection, but basically, all James I farthings look identical and would be worthy inclusions in any collection of

American Colonial coins. Since the Colonial history of these farthings stretches into the 1630's (and probably a little beyond), a Charles I harp or rose farthing would also merit inclusion in your collection.

As far as price and availability, Charles I farthings are easier to find than James I farthings as well as being somewhat less expensive. A Charles I harp or rose farthing will cost about $10-$20 in low to average circulated condition, and a James I farthing about $15-$30 in average circulated condition. A little shopping around may result in even lower prices. Do your hunting at large coin shows, with world coin mail order dealers, and of course, on eBay (use search word, "16* farthing," "James farthing" or "Charles farthing").

If you're hoping to track down a 1613 tin-coated James I farthing – don't hold your breath. These are quite rare, and if found, quite costly. A Type I farthing (without tin-coating) or Type II 1613-14 farthing is much more within the realm of possibility. It just takes some looking. Good luck!

1598-1621 Silver Patard of
Brabant, Netherlands

CHAPTER NINE

THE COINS THAT BUILT WALL STREET!

(*1570-1660 Dutch Coins*)

It's an oft-repeated story: the Dutch purchased what would become known as Manhattan Island from the local Indians in 1626 for a sum approximating $24. A lesser-known follow-up story is that the Dutch actually had one put over on them: the Indians from whom they purchased Manhattan Island actually had no real claim to the property. In fact, they were just passing through the area! What's more, to the Indian way of thinking, no one could own land anyway! If the Dutch wanted to proffer a goodwill trade that would give them the privilege of sharing the island with any other Indian tribes who wanted to live there, well, so be it. So, at the time, both sides probably felt they got the better end of the deal. From that peculiar beginning, the settlement of New Amsterdam would grow into today's "Big Apple," otherwise known as New York City.

The very first settlers of "New Netherlands" were primarily Walloons, French-speaking Protestant refugees from Flanders (now present-day Belgium). The West India Company of the Netherlands was looking for folks to settle the Dutch New World territories, and the Walloons, seeking to escape religious persecution, volunteered. So, in 1623, some thirty Walloon families sailed from Amsterdam to the New World. Upon arrival, they were dispersed over a wide area; eight families settled on Manhattan Island; two families settled in what is today Hartford, Connecticut. Twenty families settled at Fort Nassau, but moved shortly thereafter to Fort Orange, the site of present-day Albany, New York.

By 1626, it became apparent to Governor Peter Minuit that Manhattan Island was the logical trading and shipping center of New Netherlands. That being the case, Minuit called back the settlers from the Connecticut, Fort Orange and Delaware River settlements. A military garrison was maintained at Fort Orange, but the non-military settlers were quite happy to relocate to Manhattan, since surrounding native tribes seemed to be growing more menacing of late. With the recall of the outlying Walloon families from Fort Orange, the settlement of New Amsterdam ballooned to around 270.

From 1626 to 1638, New Amsterdam left much to be desired. The fort was in disrepair. The West India Company's policy of not opening trade to the public resulted in a thriving underground of smuggling and illegal trade with the Indians. It was perhaps news of the seedy reputation of New Amsterdam that discouraged large numbers of would-be Dutch settlers from coming over to New Netherlands. Finally, the West India Company was forced to loosen up and trade was opened up to the public. People could now own farm land, and, as an added incentive, free passage to the colony AND free help in clearing the fields was ALSO provided. At last the Dutch colony began to grow.

When Peter Stuyvesant became governor of New Netherlands in 1647, he immediately insisted on a civic improvement plan for New Amsterdam. Streets were paved with cobblestones; a city council was created; and nationalities from all over Europe were welcomed as residents. Immigrants from France, Denmark, Sweden, England, Germany, Poland, Portugal and even New England, made their homes in the neat Dutch houses that lined the streets of the city, or on farms along the Hudson River.

Another of Stuyvesant's projects was to erect a wall-like barrier of posts at the north end of New Amsterdam. This barrier was to protect the city from Indian raids and was known as "de wal." This long wall of posts is no longer there, but the boundary path on which it lay is today known as Wall Street!

These days, huge amounts of money change hands on Wall Street. It's kind of exciting then, to be able to obtain a genuine coin that would have been recognized and used by the first settlers of Manhattan Island— a coin that might have been among the first hard money to enter commerce on Wall Street! Probably the most famous of the New Amsterdam coins is the Dutch leeuwendaalder, struck from roughly the 1570's through the 1660's. These large silver coins were also known in Colonial America as "Lion Dollars" or "Dog Dollars" as the crouched lion on the coin obverse somewhat resembles a dog! The reverse design shows a Dutch soldier in full body armor.

The Dutch leeuwendaalder is considered by many to be America's first true "silver dollar." In fact, from the term, "daalder" evolved the term, "dollar." Although the Lion dollars were struck in the Netherlands, these coins circulated extensively throughout New Netherlands and also in the British Colonies during the 17th century. The Lion dollar also shared space in Colonial commerce with the Spanish eight reales silver cob coins.

Lion dollars are not exactly "overlooked" by collectors of American Colonial coins. When sold, they are usually trumpeted as being "America's First Dollar Coin," and it's hard to argue against that assertion. In my opinion, it is indeed worth the $70-$85 price for a low-grade specimen, or $85-$135 for an average circulated Lion dollar of the 1600's. Look for these prices to climb, but for right now, those prices seem to be holding steady.

The truly overlooked coins of early New Amsterdam are, in my opinion, the humble copper and silver coins that came over with the first settlers. Those first settlers of New Amsterdam were, of course, the Walloons. What kinds of coins might they have brought with them? The Walloons hailed from a part of the Netherlands that is today Belgium. That's why you should keep an eye out for any copper or small silver coin struck in the provinces of Brabant or Flanders. To fit into the early New Amsterdam period, these coins should date roughly 1570-1660. Of course, you'll want coins struck before 1626 if you want to imagine your coin was there when Manhattan Island was purchased from the Indians!

In truth, just about any copper or silver coin from the Netherlands dating from 1570-1660 would be worthy "Early New Amsterdam" coins, for by the 1640's a good number of Dutch settlers, not just Walloons, had sailed over to New Netherlands. A copper duit of Holland dated 1604-27 should cost only around $8-$15 in average circulated condition. A Holland silver 2 stuiver coin of 1614-28, about nickel-size in diameter, can be purchased for $15-$25 in pleasant circulated condition.

The typical U.S. coin shop is not likely to have such coins. However, they might be found at the larger American coin shows if world coin dealers are represented, and they can certainly be found on eBay. If you do look on eBay, use such search words as "Dutch," "Brabant," "Flanders,"

"Spanish Netherlands," "Duit," "Stuiver," "16* Belgium," "16* Amsterdam," or "16* Holland."

Here's another helpful eBay hint: type in the search words, "detector finds," or "dug coins." This will bring up auction listings of metal detector lots that contain old coins. Most of these metal detector lots are from the United Kingdom or the United States, but every now and then you'll find one from the Netherlands which might well contain Dutch coins from the 1500's and 1600's! These are excellent places to hunt down the very first coins of New York City!

1667 British Trade Token, "His Halfe Penny"

CHAPTER TEN

QUAKER COINAGE OF 1680'S PENNSYLVANIA

(*1649-72 British Trade Tokens*)

W hen King Charles I was beheaded in 1649, England entered her Commonwealth era, a period that lasted only twelve years. When Charles II took the throne in 1660, the succession of British kings and queens continued. During the Commonwealth years, and also a few years prior and after, no royally authorized copper coins or tokens were struck. The last royal patent farthing was struck in 1644, and there would be no official royal copper coins struck in England again until 1672.

With no official base-metal coins or tokens available to the populace for small transactions, many, MANY private farthing and halfpenny tokens were struck to meet demand throughout Great Britain from 1649 through 1672. They were generally the size of a U.S. cent or nickel in diameter and made of either copper or brass. Known today as 17th century British Trade Tokens, many of these pieces were struck by merchants, advertising their business, and others were used to advertise a particular locale.

Designs were usually simple but varied widely. In most cases, there were legends and inscriptions on one side (such as "His Halfe Penny") and initials or perhaps a simple shield of arms on the other. Some tokens featured a queen's head, a sailing ship, a human skeleton or merchandise offered by a particular merchant (i.e.,piece of clothing, a mug of ale, etc.). Most of these tokens are dated in the 1650's and 1660's.

We know these 17th century trade tokens came to the Colonies. While they may not have been plentiful, they have turned up in excavations in such places as the Tidewater area of Virginia and Long Island, New York. Perhaps most interesting is their Philadelphia and Quaker connection, for which we go back to the year of 1682.

Under King Charles II, copper farthing and halfpenny coins (particularly the farthings) were being struck in large quantities starting in 1672. In that year, the many private farthing and halfpenny tokens were demonetized and could no longer pass at face value in Great Britain. Then, in 1682, a group of some 40 Quakers secured a supply of these now-demonetized tokens. Why on earth would the Quakers want these scorned tokens? To take them to America, of course! After all, the tokens were purchased at a discount– and word had it they could be circulated in the Colonies at face value!

In fact, below is an excerpt from the London Newspaper, *The Loyal Impartial Mercury*, issue number 34, October 3-6, 1682:

From Bristol. They write that another Ship is fitting out for Pennsylvania on board which 40 Quakers together with their families will imbarq; and amongst other things tis said they carry over with them 300 pounds-worth of Half-pence and Farthings which in that Colony go currant for twice their value and 'tis added that some discontented Presbyterians will likewise accompany them.

In December of 1682, a ship named *The Unicorn* arrived in Philadelphia bearing Quakers and their supply of halfpence and farthings. Please understand, it is not DOCUMENTED that the halfpence and farthings were the trade tokens of 1649-72, but it is *believed* they were. That would make sense, as it certainly would have been profitable for the Quakers to purchase "worthless" de-monetized tokens in England only to turn around and circulate them in America at face value or more. It seems the tokens circulated not only in Pennsylvania, but in other nearby Colonies as well. At least until 1698 or so. At THAT time, a sufficient quantity of royally authorized copper coins arrived in the Colonies from Britain. It is believed the 1649-72 trade tokens were then de-valued in the American Colonies.

This brings us to the question: Of the many British Trade Tokens struck during the mid-1600's, which most likely had strong American Colonial connections? I will offer up two candidates, the first of which is a 1652-70 farthing token of Bristol. Going back to our 1682 article in the London newspaper, you'll notice that the Quakers sailed to Philadelphia from the English port city of Bristol. Hence, it would seem logical that there were many Bristol tokens among the supply of farthing and halfpence tokens. The standard design of the Bristol tokens is a sailing ship in the harbor, a castle-like structure in the background. On the reverse, the large letters, "C.B" stand for "City Of Bristol."

A little more difficult to find would be my second candidate— a trade token of Maidstone in Kent. Eight of these tokens were excavated in the Hamptons on Long Island. In addition, a Portsmouth (Hampshire) token of 1656 was uncovered in the Tidewater area of Virginia. A 17th century British Trade Token can often be purchased for $7 -$15 in lower circulated condition. For a relatively common example in average circulated condition, expect to pay around $15-$25. On eBay you can find listings for these tokens by typing in search words such as, "17th token," or "16* token." Prices seem to be going up slowly, but surely, on these pieces as they gain in popularity.

(from top, going clockwise)
1621-1746 Spanish-Colonial 2 Reales Cob, 1598-1665
Spanish-Colonial 8 Reales Cob, 1695-99 British Farthing
of William III, 1653-58 France Liard of Louis XIV

CHAPTER ELEVEN

PIRATE COINS!

I have Disneyland to thank for my deep interest in pirate coins. Yes, you probably guessed it – the Pirates of The Caribbean ride made a deep impression on me. It was, and still is, my favorite ride in the park! What could be better? You board a boat in some dark Louisiana lagoon, then drift through the quiet, sleepy swamp until you come to a brick bridge where a talking skeleton head warns, "So.. You want to be adventurin' amongst the pirates, eh?" With that, your boat plunges down a waterfall into a dark, musty cavern!

As your boat winds through the cavern tunnels, a ghostly voice croaks, "Dead men tell no tales!" Your boat proceeds to sail past underground pirate lairs and a shipwreck being steered by a skeletal crew, until finally you emerge out of the cavern into the bay of some 18th century Caribbean port! Cannonballs are fired above your head. Then, you are steered through a Caribbean town in the midst of being burned and pillaged by pirate raiders! With realistic-looking buccaneer ruffians carousing and fighting just a few feet from you, your boat finally emerges back to the friendlier Louisiana bayou where you began.

Though the Pirates of The Caribbean adventure frightened me as a child, it intrigued me as a teen. It occurred to me as I floated through the underground cavern in 1982: wouldn't it be awesome to own some genuine pirate coins! Coins that would have circulated during the Age Of Pirates! Coins that would have been struck by sea-faring nations whose vessels sailed the Spanish Main! Coins that could easily have sailed on a pirate ship!

Of course, Disneyland and a host of other commercial places long ago realized that a LOT of people think to themselves, "Wouldn't it be awesome to own pirate money!" That's why Disneyland and places with souvenir shops do a brisk business selling replicas of pirate-era coins. These replicas run the gamut from cheesy-looking to quite realistic. But they are modern reproductions, nonetheless. Most people figure that's likely as close to owning real "pirate treasure" as they're going to get! But what most people don't realize is that even the most budget-minded collector can own AUTHENTIC pirate coins! Even more amazing is the fact that a genuine pirate-era coin may cost little more (sometimes even *less*) than the cost of a modern replica!

Just what would constitute a "pirate coin?" The definition can be as loose or as strict as you like, but I will offer my suggestions. First of all, what time period are we talking about? Piracy is not limited to one particular time period. Pirates have existed since ancient times and actually still operate to this day! But come on, when we refer to the "Golden Age of Pirates," don't most of us picture the same era depicted on my favorite Disneyland ride? "The Age of Pirates," or "The Golden Age of The Buccaneers," whatever you choose to call it, was roughly 1650 to 1718. I cut it off at 1718, as that was the year the truly terrifying pirate captain, Blackbeard, was slain off the coast of North Carolina. I don't think there were many more renowned scoundrels-of-the-sea after him. A more liberal "Age of Pirates" time span would be about 1550-1730.

Second, what sea-faring countries produced pirates or were affected by piracy during this period? Spanish and Dutch ships probably suffered the most at the hands of pirates. Sailing vessels of the American Colonies were terrorized also, as in the case of Blackbeard and his crew skulking about off the Atlantic coast! But it was Spain, especially, whose treasure galleons often fell victim to piracy. After all, Spain was mining great quantities of silver and gold in the New World, striking them into cob coinage, then shipping this treasure back to Spain.

It appears that the pirate raiders were largely British and French, with some pirates coming from the American Colonies. And what may come as a surprise to many is the fact that in 1700, nearly half the pirate population were blacks! Surprising, but perhaps understandable, considering that black men enjoyed freedom and equality aboard pirate ships not found as slaves in the Colonies.

Time to get down to brass tacks. What "pirate coins" are out there, and how do you find them? Let's start off by discussing copper coins. After all, your pirate-era copper coins will be the most affordable. Can a copper coin be considered a true "pirate coin?" Again, that depends on how strict you make your definition. Certainly, a pirate wouldn't have considered a copper coin to be "treasure." Copper coins would not be good candidates for inclusion in a treasure chest. But even a pirate had to use small-denomination change when in port, and it's quite logical to assume they used copper coins for inexpensive transactions like everyone else. Remember also, pirates came from humble backgrounds, so they would have been familiar with humble copper coins. At the end of this chapter I list a few affordable pirate-era copper coins and roughly what they will cost in average circulated condition.

Silver coins, on the other hand, would indeed be considered "treasure" by a pirate. Of course, the bigger the silver coin, the more the "treasure!" The most sought-after silver coins of the pirate-era were those coined in Spanish America, as they were made of the finest silver. Of these, the undisputed king of the silver coins were "pieces of eight!" Ah, "pieces of eight," otherwise known as Spanish eight reales cobs – many people's idea of of the ultimate pirate treasure coin! A large, thick, crudely-sliced chunk of silver with the Spanish cross on one side, a shield of arms on the other, the name of this coin was continuously squawked out by the parrot in Robert Louis Stevenson's classic book, <u>Treasure Island</u>: "Pieces of Eight! Pieces of Eight!"

Spend a little more and obtain a Spanish eight reales cob. Most of those you'll encounter will date roughly 1621-1730. These coins absolutely drip with history, romance, and folklore! A lower-grade, crusty piece will cost about $50-$85, while an average grade piece will run $100-$150. Don't get too hung up over condition with these coins – they were crude and not too sharp-looking to begin with.

Maybe you need to save up for the big-sized Spanish eight reales cob. In the meantime, there are smaller, more affordable silver coins of the pirate era you can purchase. Smaller silver coins were used by pirates in the marketplace and taverns when in port. They might even have been worn by a pirate as jewelry, so keep an eye out for holed pieces! There is British silver, Spanish and Spanish-Colonial silver, Dutch silver and French silver to choose from. You might even consider a Danish silver coin of the late 1600's to early 1700's, a coin that could have been pilfered from a ship sailing to the Danish Indies!

You'll notice that I haven't mentioned gold coins in this chapter. This could be considered a glaring omission considering how much pirates coveted gold coins! Certainly there are gold coins of the pirate era out there for collectors to purchase, but I'm glossing over the gold coins, as they are not exactly low-cost items. So if you really want an authentic pirate "doubloon," be prepared to open your wallet quite a bit more!

For the truly budget-minded collector, however, I have assembled a sample list of copper and silver "pirate coins." You might call it my "pirate's dozen." Remember, this is a sample list, not an all-inclusive list. The coins listed below are, I believe, a good representation of coins that are available, affordable, and worthy heirlooms of that swashbuckling (maybe "frightening" is more like it) era! Dates are common dates for the particular coin type:

PIRATE COPPERS	Low To Average Circulated
1673 British Farthing of Charles II	$7-$18
1695-1701 British Halfpenny of William III	$7-$15
1718 British Halfpenny of George I	$8-$15
1621-65 Spanish 4 Maravedis	$6-$15
1656 France Liard of Louis XIV	$8-$20
1702 Holland Duit	$7-$15

PIRATE SILVER	
1683 British 4 Pence of Charles II	$15-$25
1696 British 6 Pence of William III	$12-$20
1722 Denmark Skilling	$10-$18
1719 Spain 2 Reales**	$20-$35
1700-46 Spanish Colonial 1 Real Cob**	$15-$25
1676 France 1/10 Ecu of Louis XIV	$20-$30

** Prices seem to be on the rise for Spanish silver in particular!

1672 British Farthing of Charles II

CHAPTER TWELVE

AFFORDABLE COINS
OF 1692 SALEM

(1672-79 British Farthings of Charles II)

One of the darkest and most sensationalized chapters in Colonial history is undoubtedly the 1692 Salem Witch Trials. In many people's minds, the very name of 'Salem' conjures up images of chaotic Puritan courtrooms packed to the hilt, where screaming and writhing young girls point their fingers at pleading old women and men, accusing them of witchcraft, as stern-faced judges and clergymen look on in horror. The accused are inevitably judged guilty of having a "familiar spirit" (demon) and sentenced to death by hanging. Without a doubt, the events that took place in Salem, Massachusetts in March of 1692 are a truly tragic and shameful chapter from our nation's past. Beginning in March 1 of 1692, a number of these trials took place in Salem. Over 150 "witches" were accused, arrested and tried. Nineteen people and two DOGS were executed, before calm and reason prevailed and the trials halted. You might well ask how the citizens of Salem could be so ignorant? How could they allow themselves to get caught up in this witch-hunting madness? It's easy for you and I to say that we would never succumb to such a fear frenzy. How easy would it be, however, to have a 21st century rationality, not to mention 300 years of historical hindsight, as a colonist of 1692 Massachusetts?

Any of you remember the popular 1999 movie, *The Blair Witch*? In this "documentary," three young film-makers hike deep into the forests of Maryland to uncover the mystery of a Colonial-era witch said to still haunt the area. The three young people are bedeviled by unseen forces as they lose their way in the woods, and it's all caught on film. Many people who went to see the movie in 1999 were truly spooked, as they were not sure if the "documentary" footage they were seeing was real or fiction. It wasn't real, but even knowing that, the *Blair Witch* movie gave millions of people the creeps. What's amazing about that is that during the entire course of the movie, there are no shots of anyone being killed, there are no dead bodies seen on camera, and the witch herself isn't even seen. Here's my challenge: watch this movie at night, then immediately proceed to a deserted forest area, and set up camp. See if your mind doesn't play a few tricks on you during the night. *The Blair Witch* is just a "documentary" movie, and a fake one at that. The colonists of 1692 Salem, Massachusetts didn't see *Blair Witch* in a movie theater – in their minds, they were living it!

The unease over dark forces and witches in Massachusetts didn't start all of a sudden in 1692. The fear had been building for some time. Here and there, strange occurrences took place, or were said to have taken place, that had no earthly explanation. People spoke of hearing disembodied voices and seeing peculiar things in the forest. Now imagine being a settler of 17th century Massachusetts and hearing through the grapevine of this following chilling incident that took place in Newbury, in 1679!

In Cotton Mather 's written account, the house of one William Morse was "infested with demons after a most horrid manner." The account goes on to tell how the home of William Morse was bombarded by brick, sticks and stones thrown by an invisible hand. William himself was attacked by invisible demons who pulled his hair, scratched his face, stole his belongings and pricked him with needles. Witnesses even saw the vision of a "black child" in the Morse house, and heard voices singing "Revenge! Revenge! Sweet is revenge!" Finally, after the Morse family prayed to God for help, there was heard the mournful cries of, "Alas! Alas! We knock no more, we knock no more!' At that point, the tormenting ceased. In the minds of the citizens of Massachusetts, there was a reason for this persecution by the forces of darkness. Clergyman Cotton Mather wrote:

The New Englanders are a people of God now settled in those parts which once were the Devil's territories, and it may be supposed that the Devil was exceedingly disturbed when he perceived such a people here. The Devil thus irritated immediately tried all sorts of methods to overturn this poor plantation.

The importance of what Mather is saying in the above text cannot be underestimated. It's a peek into the Puritan mindset and it at least gives us some semblance of under-standing as to how the 1692 Salem Witch Scare could happen. First of all, though the citizens of Salem called Salem "home," they also considered themselves to be strangers in a strange land. Massachusetts was not England. If you lived in Salem in 1692, you lived in a fairly comfort-able, civilized European-styled town. But just beyond lay untold miles of forest and wilderness where no Europeans lived, save for a few hardy frontiersmen. Sure, there were Indians, but their ways were not your ways. Some of the Indian tribes were friendly to the colony, but some were not. Then come nightfall, you talk about DARK! This was a land with few lights. You didn't venture outside the confines of town at night- who knows what lurked out in the dark forests beyond the town walls. In fact, for many Puritans, the wilderness beyond the city limits was a mysterious land inhabited by the Devil and his demons!

Secondly, the Puritans often described their colony as a "City On A Hill." In other words, the Massachusetts Puritan settlements were to be beacons of proper Christianity in the New World. And it wasn't just the Native Americans who needed a Christian "City On A Hill" to look up to and emulate. The more worldly and materialistic British settlers to the south, such as the Virginia colonists, the Spanish in Florida, the French in the Mississippi Valley and up in New France -THEY would do well to model their Colonies on the Puritan life style as well! Of course, nothing makes the Devil angrier than a people who take it upon themselves to establish a Christian city on a hill in a territory the Devil supposedly once owned, lock-stock and barrel! So, when strange and unearthly things start occurring within the colony, you, as a Massachusetts Bay colonist, kinda know why.

Sadly, the result was innocent citizens of Salem being accused, jailed, and hanged, with one man pressed to death beneath a weight of stones. Thankfully, the clergy and magistrates, admitting and repenting of their part in the witch hunt tragedy, ended the persecutions before the year's end. But the awful legacy of 1692 Salem lives on today. The site of the 1692 witch trials accounts for a large part of the tourist trade in modern-day Salem, Massachusetts. The town of Salem is today a haven for self-pronounced "witches" who no doubt feel a certain kinship with their 17th century brethren and sisters who were executed — even though it's highly doubtful that any of those put to death in 1692 Salem were directly involved with witchcraft. Famous plays and movies have been written about the infamous witch trials, the most recent being a 1996 major motion picture entitled, *The Crucible*, based on the play of the same name. It is one of the few events of late 17th century America that even the person on the street has heard about. Now for the key question (numismatically, not historically speaking). What coins were circulating on the streets of 1692 Salem, Massachusetts?

COINS OF 1692 SALEM

Picture that packed Salem courthouse of March, 1692. Picture the Puritan-era clothes, the din in the courthouse from terrified onlookers, the "bewitched" girls falling and writhing on the floor, the judges yelling, "She hath a familiar spirit!" Ok, it's not a pleasant picture. But now picture this: in the midst of the courtroom pandemonium, a few coins fall from pockets or coin purses, clanking onto the wooden floorboards. What do those coins look like?

Let's start with the obvious. In late 17th century Massachusetts, it's a good bet that an oft-seen coin would be a 17th century Massachusetts Bay Colony silver coin. These crudely hammered silver coins featuring sickly-looking oak, willow and pine trees as design devices, were struck from 1652 to roughly 1682 (even though all are dated '1652' to get around a royal decree forbidding the colony to strike her own coins AFTER that date). That means by the time 1692 rolled around, some 30 years worth of Massachusetts Bay Colony shillings, sixpence and other smaller denominations were floating around the streets of Boston, Plymouth, Salem, and other New England settlements. That would be your most obvious choice of "Coin of 1692 Salem." The problem is that today, any Massachusetts silver coin of 1652-82 falls into the category of very scarce and very expensive. With any luck, you can get a heavily worn and damaged one in the $800-$1,000 range. Happily, there are more affordable alternatives.

Certainly there were Spanish silver coins floating around Salem in 1692. This Spanish silver would have been mostly Spanish-Colonial silver cobs (basically, crude slices of silver stamped with a Spanish cross/shield of arms design) of varying denominations. It's absolutely possible to find an affordable ($20-$35) low to average circulated Spanish silver cob dated around or before 1692, especially if you're willing to settle for the smaller half real or one real cobs. The problem with these cobs, however, is pinning them down to a date. The date is rarely fully or even partially visible. Many times it's difficult to even pin down a given cob to the 17th or 18th century!

It's also safe to assume there were British coins circulating on the streets of Salem in 1692. They would be mostly coppers, since any silver and gold British coinage was usually swiftly returned to Britain as payment for British goods. So this should be easy – what were the current circulating British copper coins of 1692? Well, they would have been halfpennies and farthings of William and Mary! But not so fast. The farthings and halfpennies of William and Mary struck 1689-92 were struck in relatively small numbers and are, in fact, pretty scarce today. One reason for their scarcity today, is that these coins were struck in TIN, not copper! A goodly portion of that relatively small number minted, deteriorated over the years (tin doesn't hold up nearly as well as copper). In fact, Britain wouldn't resume striking farthings and halfpence in copper until 1694. All of this is to say I think it's doubtful that any significant number of William and Mary coins ever showed up in 1692 Salem. British silver coins of William and Mary would seldom have been seen; the mintage of the British tin farthings and halfpence was too small.

How about British farthings and halfpence just prior to William and Mary, namely those struck under James II? Here again, the 1685-87 farthings and halfpence of James II were struck in tin. Here too, they were struck in relatively small numbers, and surviving examples of that number are hard to track down today. Again, I think the sighting of James II's tin coinage in Salem, in or just prior to 1692, was a pretty rare occurrence. In fact, I don't know of any tin William and Mary or James II coins that have come out of the ground at American Colonial sites.

I do think there is one particular British copper coin that was commonly seen in 1692 Salem, Massachusetts: the humble 1672-79 copper farthing of Charles II. You might note that these coppers were struck some 20 years prior to 1692. True, but the 1672-79 Charles II farthings were struck in large numbers. They were sturdy, high-quality coppers that held up over time. They saw considerable usage, over long periods, considering how many well-worn Charles II farthings survive today. The 1672-79 farthings still commonly turn up as England metal detecting ground finds. We know they did come over to Colonial America, as some have been found at Colonial sites. One appeared in the trash pit of a Williamsburg, Virginia home that burned in 1730. These farthings were popular and well-used in Britain; it's safe to surmise that a decent number crossed the Atlantic to the Colonies as well.

Now for the good news you were expecting: the 1672-79 Charles II farthings are cheap. They are very available. I see them sold on eBay under the U.S.: COLONIALS category, in the ENGLAND: FARTHINGS category and in the metal-detecting-find lots! Some good search words would be: "16* farthing," "Charles II* farthing," "dug* coin*" (for groups of old coins dug up in England, where Charles II coppers are often found). Prices? Currently, a low circulated piece can be had for as little as $5, while $10-$20 should be enough to obtain an average circulated piece.

A 1692 ALTERNATIVE TO THE 1672-79 FARTHING

What about the Charles II farthings of the 1680's? They were struck in much smaller numbers, so it's doubtful very many came over to America. What about the Charles II copper halfpennies? They were only struck for four years, 1672-75, and in far fewer numbers than the farthings. They are quite hard to find these days. There is a coin that, I believe, is also a worthy "Coin of 1692 Salem" candidate, one that gets you right up to the year of 1692! This coin would be the 1692 Irish halfpenny of William and Mary. These pieces were struck in copper and in much greater numbers that the British tin halfpennies and farthings of 1692. As Irish copper coins came over to Colonial America nearly as often as British copper coins, I believe Salem, Massachusetts saw its share of William and Mary Irish halfpence in commerce. As far as availability today, you won't find them on the market nearly as often as you will the 1672-79 British farthings, but they do appear for sale from time to time. When they do come up for sale, they can often be purchased for around $15-25 for a low circulated piece, or problem average circulated piece (holed, bent, etc).

1672-75 British Halfpenny of Charles II & 1699
British Halfpenny of William III

CHAPTER THIRTEEN

WILL AMERICA'S FIRST LARGE CENT PLEASE STAND UP?

(British Halfpennies of Charles II And William III)

Many collectors consider the 1793 Chain cent to be our nation's first large cent. The 1787 Fugio cent is also widely considered to be our nation's first large cent, even though it wasn't struck by the United States Mint (though it was authorized by the United States government). All right, both of the above answers are technically correct. But I will assert that the 1793 Chain cent and the 1787 Fugio cent had a Colonial forerunner: the British halfpenny.

Before we go further, let's clear up a few things. Our nation's first large cents were not the equivalent of a British halfpenny. Our nation's "one cent" coins did not evolve directly from British pence or halfpence. I know, many will say the U.S. large cents eventually became Indian Head and Lincoln "pennies," but "penny" is an incorrect term for those one-cent coins you have piling up in a jar. A "pence" is not the same as a "cent." Denomination comparisons between countries can get awfully complex, so just trust me on that one. The U.S. large cent, being thicker and heavier than the British halfpence of Colonial times, had more purchasing power.

So how can a British halfpenny be the forerunner of our nation's large cent? Well, it's only my theory, but let me explain it this way. If you were shopping for supplies in 1800 Philadelphia, and the asking price for an item was "two coppers," you would probably pay the merchant with two U.S. large cents. If you were shopping for supplies in 1750 Philadelphia, and the asking price for an item was "two coppers," you would pay the merchant with two British halfpennies. The large cent was the primary copper coin of the early United States; the British halfpence was the primary copper coin of Colonial America – or at least 1695 to 1787 America! Prior to 1695, there simply was no copper coinage that consistently showed up in Colonial commerce! In 1698, all that changed, but more on that later..

First, a brief history of the British halfpenny. The halfpenny or halfpence, was first introduced in England around the early 1300's. But it wasn't a copper coin, it was a small silver coin. The tiny silver halfpenny was a fairly consistent, but not terribly prominent coin denomination from the 1300's to the mid-1600's. That changed radically during the reign of Charles II. In 1672, Charles II introduced a NEW halfpenny in the form of a large-sized copper coin. This new halfpence was a good deal larger in diameter than our present-day U.S. quarter. Or, as another comparison, about the same size in diameter as the later U.S. large cents of 1793-1857!

Yes, just as the Spanish Milled eight reales silver coins of the 1700's influenced the first U.S. silver dollars, there's no question that the British halfpennies of 1672-1775 influenced the American state coppers of 1785-88, and later, the U.S. large cents of 1793-1857. The early U.S. large cents may have been heavier than the Colonial-era British halfpennies, but the size of the coins were roughly the same. In fact, the 1780's state copper coins of Connecticut, Vermont and New York strongly resembled 1730-75 British halfpennies of George II and George III!

Did those first copper halfpennies of Charles II come over to Colonial America? It would be logical to assume they did, but I don't know of any specific Charles II halfpennies that have turned up in excavations. I feel very comfortable in asserting that probably few colonists got their hands on the Charles II halfpennies. It appears that few were struck, which would account for their present scarcity. What you WILL find, are plenty of Charles II farthings! So, in short, either few Charles II were struck, or for some reason, few survive.

Likewise, there is no documented or archaeological evidence that the copper halfpennies of James II (ruled 1685-88) or William & Mary (ruled jointly 1688-94) found their way to Colonial America in any kind of significant number. This brings us to 1698. Now, if you recall in the chapter on British trade tokens, it was around 1698 that privately-struck farthing and halfpenny tokens were de-valued in the American Colonies. This was due largely to a shipment of OFFICIAL royal copper coins that arrived in the Colonies that year. These coppers were British halfpennies and farthings of William III – mostly halfpennies.

William III was the sole monarch of Great Britain from 1694 to 1702. From 1688 to 1694, William ruled jointly with his wife, Mary (ever hear of the Virginia college of William And Mary?).William III deposed King James II once and for all in the "Glorious Revolution" of 1690, a power struggle that ended without bloodshed. The most visible legacy of King William III in our country is, undoubtedly, Colonial Williamsburg in Virginia. Founded in 1699, Williamsburg became the capitol of Virginia when it was decided that the seat of government would be relocated from burnt-out Jamestown.

What was making headlines in the Colonies when the William III coppers were in circulation? In 1699, the Abenaki Indians and the Massachusetts colonists signed a treaty, finally ending their conflict. Out west, the Louisiana territory was being settled by some 200 French colonists, the first Europeans to settle that region. Also in 1699, yellow fever swept through the Philadelphia area, killing 1/6 of the population. Out on the seas, gentleman buccaneer Captain William Kidd preyed on cargo ships. Kidd was at finally caught, tried and hanged in New York City. And in 1704, Queen Anne's War in Europe spread to the New World, where British settlers battled the French and their Indian allies on the frontier.

As for the William III halfpennies themselves, we know they did indeed circulate on the streets of late 17th and early 18th century Philadelphia. William III coppers have been excavated at Philadelphia road construction sites, and elsewhere in Pennsylvania, such as Hannah Town and Fort Ligonier sites. Furthermore, these coppers received mention in mid-1700's Colonial news journals of Boston and New York. These articles reported that William III coppers had been in circulation for decades. These articles ALSO reported William III halfpence being amongst the proliferation of counterfeited coins plaguing Colonial commerce! Now folks, when a particular coin or paper money receives special attention from counterfeiters, that's proof positive of a coin or paper money's influence in the marketplace!

So why am I talking so much about the William III halfpennies when the Charles II halfpennies were clearly the first halfpennies to come over to America? A valid question. After all, the Charles II halfpennies WERE the first large-cent-sized coppers coins of Britain to show up here, even though I have yet to see concrete proof of that. Still, logic dictates that at least a FEW must have come over – and if at least a few did, then the Charles II halfpenny is the first large cent forerunner to make its appearance in the United States! In short, the 1672-75 halfpence is our nation's first "large cent."After all, there's only one winner in a race, right?

Yes and no. For while the Charles II halfpenny can be called our nation's first large cent in the technical sense, I believe the William III halfpenny is our first large cent in the practical sense – the first British halfpenny to truly proliferate in Colonial commerce. So which one should you go for? I say, go for BOTH – that way, you'll have all bases covered. As stated many times in this chapter, the Charles II halfpenny is hard to find. Difficult as they are to track down, however, prices don't seem to be outrageous. A low to average circulated piece can still be purchased for $25-$40. In my opinion, that's a huge bargain for such a scarce and historical coin! But it will take some looking. By far your best bet (especially if you don't live in the United Kingdom) is to search on eBay by typing in the search words, "charles II halfp*."

Now for the really good <u>news:</u> halfpennies of William III are readily available on the market. Prices are still LOW for low to average circulated pieces! They are OFTEN overlooked, passed over by collectors (doesn't that sound like a consistent theme in this book?). In on-line auctions, I've seen average circulated William III halfpennies go unsold at a $5 opening bid! In fact, low-circulated William III halfpennies and farthings often go begging for buyers – even at prices of $5 and under. But lay aside $7-$15 for a low to average circulated piece. Prices go up sharply for circulated pieces with nicer detail. Expect to pay $25-$45 for higher-grade pieces. And if you ever do get a chance to visit Colonial Williamsburg (a must for every American history lover), I can't think of a better coin to carry around in your pocket!

I'll say it plainly: you need one of these 17th century halfpennies in your collection! Even if you don't buy my theory that they are our nation's earliest large cent, there is no denying their place in Colonial coinage history! These coppers were "workhorse" coins – they were more apt to be spent than saved. Colonists tended to spend their coppers and save their silver and gold (if they could manage to keep their silver and gold out of the hands of the tax collector)! And when you compare the price of a 1698 British halfpenny with the price of a 1793 U.S. Chain cent, you'll see what a bargain these old halfpennies are!

CHAPTER FOURTEEN

THE COPPERS THAT HELPED BENJAMIN FRANKLIN 'COIN" A PHRASE

If you ask most people to name some of America's most notable "Founding Fathers," three names in particular will likely be offered up: George Washington, Thomas Jefferson and the man we will be discussing in this chapter: Benjamin Franklin. Even the most history-challenged amongst us have heard of Benjamin Franklin — if only because he flew a kite during a lightning storm, got himself zapped, and in the process, discovered electricity. Yes, Benjamin Franklin pulled off a dangerous stunt, but he did much more than that in his extraordinary life. In the course of his 84 years, Franklin rose from humble beginnings to become an expert printer, a witty journalist, an accomplished scientist, an able musician, a renowned diplomat, an inventor and a much-quoted philosopher. His intellect and revolutionary zeal helped spark our nation's drive for independence. In short, Benjamin Franklin was a genius.

It would take a full book to document Franklin's life and achievements. This chapter, however, will focus on one of

Franklin's most famous quotations: "Don't give too much for the whistle." If you aren't familiar with that particular phrase, you should be. That simple little proverb is filled with far-reaching wisdom, and is as true today as it was when Franklin first spoke it in the 18th century. Here is how it came about, in Franklin's own words:

> *When I was a child of seven years old, my friends, on a holiday, filled my pocket with coppers. I went directly to a shop where they sold toys for children; and, being charmed with the sound of a whistle, that I met by the way in the hands of another boy, I voluntarily offered and gave all my money for one. I then came home, and went whistling all over the house, much pleased with my whistle, but disturbing all the family. My brothers, and sisters, and cousins, understanding the bargain I had made, told me I had given four times as much for it as it was worth; put me in mind what good things I might have bought with the rest of the money; and laughed at me so much for my folly, that I cried with vexation; and the reflection gave me more chagrin than the whistle gave me pleasure. This however was afterwards of use to me, the impression continuing on my mind; so that often, when I was tempted to buy some unnecessary thing, I said to myself, Don't give too much for the whistle; and I saved my money.*

Franklin goes on to give examples of people who wind up "paying too much for their whistle":

> *If I knew a miser, who gave up every, kind of comfortable living, all the pleasure of doing good to others, all the esteem of his fellow-citizens, and the joys of benevolent friendship, for the sake of accu-*

mulating wealth, Poor man, said I, you pay too much for your whistle.

When I met with a man of pleasure, sacrificing every laudable improvement of the mind, or of his fortune, to mere corporeal sensations, and ruining his health in their pursuit, Mistaken man, said I, you are providing pain for yourself, instead of pleasure; you give too much for your whistle.

If I see one fond of appearance, or fine clothes, fine houses, fine furniture, fine equipages, all above his fortune, for which he contracts debts, and ends his career in a prison, Alas! say I, he has paid dear, very dear, for his whistle.

Now you know a little bit about Benjamin Franklin and his famous "whistle" quote. But just what does this have to do with coins? Glad you asked. If you read Franklin's account again, you'll notice that he makes reference to a "pocket filled with coppers." And just what were these "coppers?"' Why, copper coins of course. Now you see where we're going with this, don't you? Young Benjamin Franklin gave up all his copper coins– probably all or most of his monetary treasure at the time– for the whistle he coveted, the same whistle he later regretted purchasing at too great a price. The key question: just what were those copper coins that helped coin the immortal phrase "Don't give too much for the whistle?"

The whistle story takes place when Benjamin Franklin was seven years old. Given that Franklin was born in 1706, that means young Ben bought his whistle in 1713, or possibly 1714. And what kind of copper coins would seven year-old Ben be carrying around in Colonial America in 1713 or 1714? Right away, we can eliminate the possibility that they were American-made Colonial copper coins. There was no such thing in 1713-14. There is the possibility that a couple of those copper coins were French or Dutch, but in all likelihood the coppers were British. So let's go on that assumption.

Unfortunately, Franklin doesn't give us any details as to the nature of his copper coins. That means we'll have to do some educated guesswork. At the time, there were two types of British copper coins, the halfpence and the farthing. Which denomination would young Ben have been carrying? I have a feeling his stash of coppers consisted of farthings AND halfpennies. One could make the argument that only the humblest of coins would be found in the pockets of a seven year-old boy in Colonial America, that being the farthing. On the other hand, British halfpennies were the most commonly encountered coppers of Colonial America. Perhaps the safest guess, then, is that young Ben paid for his whistle with farthings as well as halfpennies.

Now that we know we're working with British farthings and halfpennies, let's try and narrow it down further. What would those farthings and halfpennies have looked like? That question is followed by the next obvious question: what monarchs ruled in 1713 and 1714? In 1713, Queen Anne was Britain's monarch. She also ruled through some of 1714, but died before the year was over. King George I began his rule in that same year of 1714. Does that mean young Ben's copper coin stash consisted of farthings and halfpence of Anne and George I? Almost certainly, the answer to that is a resounding NO!

First of all, there were virtually no coppers struck during the reign of Queen Anne. I say virtually none because there was a tiny mintage of Queen Anne farthings in 1714. But that mintage was so small it's unlikely that even a handful ever reached the Colonies, much less young Benjamin Franklin's pocket! As for King George I, true, he did begin his reign in 1714, but no coppers were struck under his monarchy until 1717. That would rule out any copper farthings or halfpence of Queen Anne or George I being our Ben Franklin "whistle" coins.

That leaves us with the earlier British monarchs who coined coppers: William III (1694-1702), William and Mary (1689-94), James II (1685-90), and Charles II (1660-84). We'll start with the earliest of these monarchs and work our way forward.

CHARLES II (1660-85): Though Charles II's reign began in 1660, official copper coins were not struck under his rule until 1672. The vast majority of copper coins struck under Charles II were farthings. Charles II also struck copper halfpence, but they must have been struck in far smaller number than the farthings, as it is quite a rare occurrence to encounter a Charles II halfpenny today. That's not the case with Charles II farthings-these nickel-sized coppers are still fairly easy to obtain.

JAMES II (1685-88):   Farthings and halfpence from the reign of James II are seldom encountered. They were indeed struck, but apparently in small numbers judging from their scarcity today. What's more, James II tried to save money and appease the tin producers of Britain by striking his farthings in TIN, not copper! James II DID, however, issue a significant emergency copper and brass coinage in Ireland from 1689-90. This mostly brass coinage is known as "Gun Money" as these pieces were supposedly made from melted down cannons.

WILLIAM & MARY (1689-94): The copper coinage was kicked up a bit when King William III and his queen, Mary, took the throne. Some tin farthings and halfpence were struck early on, but in 1694, there was a fairly healthy production of pure copper farthings and halfpence, featuring the jugate (side by side) busts of William and Mary on the obverse.

WILLIAM III (1694-1702): When Queen Mary died in 1694, William III was left to rule Britain alone. Under William's reign, there was an even greater output of copper farthings and halfpence, featuring, of course, the lone bust of William on the obverse.

We now know the monarchs, so which monarch's coppers would have paid for young Ben Franklin's historic whistle? Let's begin by remembering that, in 1713-14, NO coin was circulating in America in huge numbers. Still, I think it's safe to say that a coin that was commonly encountered in Britain would have been MOST likely to have turned up in Colonial America. By the same token, any coin that was seldom encountered in Britain would have been a true rarity in Colonial America. So let's start off by eliminating the copper and tin coins struck in Britain in small numbers: the Charles II halfpence, any farthing or halfpence of James II, and any farthing or halfpence of William & Mary struck prior to 1694.

That leaves the Charles II farthing, struck in large numbers. That leaves the William & Mary farthing and halfpence of 1694, struck in fairly large numbers, but only in that one year, mind you. That leaves the farthings and halfpence of William III—- both struck in large numbers. And the winner is....the copper farthings and halfpence of William III.

It's not just that the coppers of William III were struck in large numbers compared to earlier reigns. A large number of William III coppers came to America in 1698, the first significant shipment of copper coins from Britain to America ever (more on that in another chapter). In fact, I would venture to say that most, if not all of young Ben Franklin's coppers were farthings and halfpennies of William III.

Even though it's likely that most, maybe all, of young Ben's coppers were William III pieces, we cannot discount another monarch or monarchs being in that grouping that bought the whistle. To round out a grouping of Young Ben Franklin coppers, I would include a Charles II farthing or two, even though these coins were some 40 years old by 1713-14. I say that because there do seem to be as many Charles II farthings floating around today as William III farthings or halfpence. That would seem to point to an enormous output of these 1672-79 farthings. And lastly, we don't know how MANY coppers young Ben was carrying with him the day he bought his whistle. For the sake of argument, let's just say it was a dozen. So, to sum it up, below is my personal (but very unscientific) "Ben Franklin's Whistle" dozen:

3 William III Farthings
6 William III Halfpennies
2 Charles II Farthings
1 William & Mary Halfpenny

Any one of the above halfpence or farthings can currently be purchased one eBay, at a coin show, or a coin shop, for roughly $10-$25 in low to average circulated condition. The William and Mary halfpence would be the most expensive and hardest to find. I won't delve too deeply into pricing, as the William III and Charles II coppers are discussed in more detail in other chapters.

CHAPTER FIFTEEN

POCKET & PURSE CHANGE OF 1700's COLONIAL AMERICA

In the 1600's, the few coins circulating in Colonial America were a hodge-podge of copper, silver, and gold coins from other countries, with the mid-1600's silver coinage of Massachusetts being the only major exception. By the 1700's, coins were more common in the streets of Colonial America, but they were still not plentiful. Coinage of good copper, and especially silver and gold, were most welcome in the Colonies, even if these coins filtered in from Mexico, Peru, Bolivia, England, France, Spain, the Netherlands, Portugal or the German States! It's just that by the mid-1700's, there was more of a pattern established as to what types of coins the typical American colonist was likely to encounter.

By the pivotal year of 1776, a few general rules now applied when to came to your pocket change. Namely that, by and large, your silver coins are Spanish. And those Spanish silver coins will usually be Spanish-Colonial issues, with a few silver coins from the Spanish mainland thrown in for good measure. This rule-of-thumb seems to have been reversed in Colonial Williamsburg, but more on that in another chapter.

As a citizen of Colonial America, the vast majority of your copper coins are British – some are farthings, but most of your coppers are halfpennies of George II or George III. What's more, nearly half or more of the British coppers that cross your palm will be counterfeit! What few gold coins you'll encounter will be a smattering of Spanish, British, Dutch or Portuguese pieces.

The coinage picture in America will change radically by the late 1700's. By the mid-1780's, the Revolutionary War is over, America has achieved her independence and is now self-governing. It is time for a true American coinage, and it does indeed appear in 1785, when a few states act on their new-found right to strike their own coins. The state of Connecticut strikes her own copper coins, followed soon after by New Jersey, New York, Massachusetts. Vermont also strikes her own coinage, though when they begin to do so in 1785, they are actually their own republic, not a state. British copper coins still circulate outside the population centers, but by and large, British farthings and halfpence are yesterday's news. As for the change in silver and gold coinage by the 1780's... well, there is no change, really.

Though some of the states are now producing fairly large numbers of copper coins, none of the states are striking silver coins. Consequently, Spanish silver coins still rule in American commerce and will CONTINUE to do so into the 1800's, long after the U.S. Mint has been established. Speaking of establishing a national mint, by 1787, our nation has finally moved from being a confederacy of states, to becoming the Unites States of America. But a United States mint is still six years away from becoming a reality. And if you'll remember from early in the book, the 1787 Fugio cent was authorized by the newly formed United States Congress. James Jarvis, the private contractor charged with striking the Fugio cent, does not deliver nearly as many coins as was authorized by the government.

Finally, in 1793, the United States Mint begins operation in Philadelphia. American coinage will see yet another transformation of its daily coinage. Now, instead of British farthings and halfpence, instead of state copper coins, there are official U.S. half cents and large cents appearing on the streets! But our coinage will continue to evolve throughout 1793: that first year of operation, our nation's large cent goes through THREE major design changes!

In 1794, the U.S. Mint begins striking the first U.S. silver coins: half dimes, half dollars and dollars. In 1795, our first gold coins are struck. What does all this mean? It means that someone like George Washington, who was born in 1732 and dies in 1799, has seen a staggering array of Colonial, state and United States coinage in their lifetime!

We'll be discussing a number of specific 18th century issues that saw notable action in America. However, below, I have compiled a short representative sample set of coins often seen in the Thirteen Colonies around 1776. The coins listed below are all very available and affordable. They would make for an impressive mini-museum of Colonial monetary history! I've listed approximate retail prices as of 2006. Knock off a few dollars for pieces that have sustained some damage.

1770-75 British Farthing of George III
$7-$15 in average circulated condition

1730-59 British Halfpenny of George II
$5-$12 in average circulated condition

1770-87 Counterfeit Halfpenny - George III type
$5-$25 in average circulated condition

1732-70 Spanish-Colonial Pillar Type 1/2 Real
$20-$35 in average circulated condition

1700-46 Spanish 1 Real
$12-$20 in low to average circulated condition

Obverse of Counterfeit British Farthing, 1770-75 Type

CHAPTER SIXTEEN

A PAUSE TO DISCUSS COUNTERFEITS

*(Small-Change Scourge of The
Colonies and Great Britain)*

T hough I'm not going to highlight any piece in particular, no discussion of Colonial and early American coins is complete without touching on the subject of counterfeits. Not modern counterfeits, mind you, but 18th and early 19th century counterfeits. These pieces are significant, since it's estimated that nearly half or MORE of all British coppers circulating in the Colonies were British or American-made evasions and forgeries!

If you have been paying attention, you will recall that the copper coins of King William III were the first British coins to sail over to American in any kind of quantity. Then – VOILA– the first counterfeit coppers to appear in any quantity: William III halfpenny counterfeits! But by far and away the most common counterfeits of 1700's America were of

George II and George III halfpennies. There were also farthing counterfeits, but not as much as the phony halfpence.

These early American fakes are a fascinating study. The number and variety of types recorded is mind-boggling and enough to keep any specialist busy researching for a lifetime! If you do decide to purse an in-depth study of these privately-made forgeries, a must-have resource is The Forgotten Coins of North America by William Anton and Bruce Kesse. For right now, however, you might want to simply know how to spot a counterfeit copper.

First of all, counterfeit coppers were struck in the British Isles and in America throughout the 1700's and into the early 1800's. Even today, there is much debate over which particular counterfeit coppers were struck in Britain and which were struck in America. True, some well-known types can be traced specifically to American or British makers. However, we are still in the dark as to the origin of a host of other types.

The best way I know to spot a counterfeit, is to handle and scrutinize the genuine article! Study an official George II halfpence – how does the bust portrait look? Weight-wise, how does it feel in the palm of your hand? What seems to be the standard thickness for official George II coppers? Note the craftsmanship of the design, of the lettering. If you are familiar with the official coins, then counterfeits are much easier to spot. Below are some key things to look for in a Colonial/early American counterfeit coin (keep in mind, that while these are general rules, they apply mostly to the farthing and halfpence forgeries that flooded the streets of 18th century Britain and America).(1) SMALL/ LIGHTWEIGHT PLANCHET: Oftentimes, the counterfeit is slightly smaller in diameter than the official regal counterpart. Also, it is usually thinner and lighter than the official coin. This is particularly true of many fake farthings, some of which are almost wafer-thin!

(2) BOGUS LEGENDS: The legend on an official 1770-75 George III halfpence or farthing reads, "Georgius III.Dei. Gratia" on the obverse; "Britan.nia" on the reverse. Suppose you come across what appears to be a 1770-75 halfpence, but the legend reads, "England Forever," or "Guilliemus Shakespeare," or "Claudius Romulus!" What you have here is a definite counterfeit, and almost certainly a British counterfeit! These farthings and halfpence with the bogus legends are commonly referred to as "evasions," because the counterfeiter could evade prosecution on the grounds that the official coin wasn't copied thanks to the phony legend! What often differentiates an American copper counterfeit from a British copper counterfeit, is that the American phony coin will have the standard, "Georgius III.Dei Gratia/Britannia" legend. The British evasions with the bogus legends are NOT, however, to be confused with the American state coppers of the 1780's which had British designs but legends referring to the state (such as "Nova Eborac" or "Connec."). And if all this sound confusing, it is!

(3) BOGUS DATES: A phony date is the best clue that a 1770-75 George III halfpence or farthing is not what is appears to be. The same goes for the George II coppers. It's pretty cut and dried here – if you have a George III halfpence showing a date of 1776, 1778, 1787, etc., then you know your halfpence is not an official 1770-75 George III halfpence. It's either a counterfeit or an official American state copper (some of which actually AREN'T official, but we won't get into that)! Remember too, any date on a counterfeit coin is suspect: that 1776-dated piece may actually have been struck in 1785; the counterfeit halfpence showing a bust of George II may have been struck twenty years after his death!

(4) CRUDE CRAFTSMANSHIP: What will usually leap out at you is the crude artwork on many counterfeits. Here

again, being familiar with the real deal makes spotting a fake much easier. Some counterfeits were pretty well-made, and closely resemble the genuine article. Many others, however, feature almost cartoon-ish renderings of George II or George III; Miss Britannia on the reverse might resemble little more than a stick figure! Generally speaking, the counterfeit coppers struck in America and Canada (yes, they circulated there too) are more crude and cartoonish than British-made counterfeits.

Why were there so many counterfeit farthings and halfpence in the 18th century? Simply put, there was a huge demand for small change, and there were not enough good copper coins in circulation. This was especially true in Colonial and early America. Though counterfeit coppers were not exactly popular here, many merchants tolerated them because they were at least some form of hard money. It was not until around the 1820's that counterfeit coppers were finally driven from circulation in America thanks to a sufficient number of official large cents and half cents being struck by the U.S. Mint.

Because there is so much research still to do on 18th and early 19th century counterfeits, this is an area where you, the average collector, can acquire truly scarce treasures for less than the price of a matinee movie, even without the popcorn and soda! It's not uncommon for counterfeit coppers from the 1700's to show up in coin dealer junk boxes! To many dealers they simply resemble worn-out 18th century British coppers, nothing too special. Your careful eye, however, could identify that worn-out copper as a definite counterfeit, maybe even a rare American counterfeit! Such a piece would certainly be worth more than a few dollars, especially if it could be attributed.

I should also mention another type of counterfeit that turned up in late 18th century and early 19th century America:

Spanish-Colonial two reales made of brass. It is believed these counterfeits were originally lightly silvered. Some experts also believe these pieces were made and circulated in New York, but some believe they are of Canadian manu-facture. The Spanish brass counterfeits are much scarcer than the bogus British coppers. These brass pieces have the same design, same legends as the Charles III and Charles IV coins they usually imitate. The design and style of legend lettering are usually fairly crude, however. Every now and then, a dealer will sell these pieces, again, thinking they are worn-out Spanish Colonial 2 reales of lesser value, and not taking much notice of its brassy appearance.

Don't overlook these historical fakes for your collec-tion! Don't look on them as you would a modern replica or fake. Modern replicas are meant to be souvenirs (or at least they SHOULD be), and by law, "COPY" must be marked on the face of them. Modern fakes are worse – they are struck to fool collectors, and will obviously NOT have "COPY" marked on them. By contrast, the old bogus British coppers and the brass Spanish coins were meant to circulate as money by their crafty makers, during roughly the same period as the genuine article circulated. Believe me, whether they knew it or not, our founding fathers passed along a healthy handful of counterfeit coins!

**Note: Ebay has recently cracked down on any listing with the word "counterfeit" in the title, even though old contempo-rary counterfeits are a legitimate collecting field. To get around this, sellers often use words like "imitation," "evasion," or "forgery" (how that slips by so often, I don't know), to describe 18th century counterfeits.

A variety of bent, holed and counter-stamped
coins of the 17th and 18th centuries

CHAPTER SEVENTEEN

BENT, HOLED & VANDALIZED

(Damaged "Junk" Coins
Could Actually Be Historic Treasure!)

When it comes to intelligent coin collecting, there is a prevailing school of thought that says, "FLEE from problem coins!" And what are problem coins? A worn coin isn't actually a problem coin, unless the wear is excessive. In fact, "just good honest wear" is a selling point for many old coins. No, problem coins are basically coins that have been cleaned, holed, bent, dented, chipped, split, etc. You get the picture-and it oftentimes ain't pretty.

You can call them "problem" coins. You can call them "damaged" coins. Either way, a purist will tell you that such pieces have lost most or all of their value - such pieces are rarely worth keeping. They have a point. Say you purchase a coin that grades Very Fine for wear, at a Very Fine retail price, but that coin also has a hole drilled through the center. Guess what? You're not going to get Very Fine money for that coin when it comes time to re-sell. You may be able to sell it, but the buyer will probably ask for a significant discount due to the hole. If you're lucky, a bidder on eBay will overlook the hole and still put in a strong bid, but don't count on it.

Of course, throughout this book, I've given you the OK to pursue the historical coins of early America, even if they have a chipped rim, a small hole at the top, a slight bend, or some greenish corrosion. Why? Because, first of all, I'm not touting these coins as "investments." Secondly, I feel the history of such coins enrich the owner's collection far more than the coin's "problems" detract from its retail market value. In other words, when I hold a worn George II halfpenny in my hands, I know I may only be able to re-sell it for $3 or so. But I also feel that this same coin contains a wealth of history that is beyond price.

Now comes the interesting part. Especially when it comes to coins from the Colonial and early American periods, sometimes the value of a coin is actually enhanced BECAUSE of a "problem!" I'm not just talking about the historical value, I'm talking about the re-sale value as well! True, a purist may still argue that damage is damage or that a problem-coin is still a problem-coin, but not all coin buyers are condition purists. Many a collector DESIRES the story that the "damage" reflects. Rather than keep circling the subject, let's see some examples.

BENT BRITISH SIXPENCE: Also known as "Witch Pieces" or "Lucky Pieces." During the 1600's and early 1700's, bending your silver sixpence seems to have been a popular pastime for British citizens, both in Britain and in the Colonies. This practice of bending the sixpence seems to have been especially prevalent during the late 1600's; consequently, you'll find that a goodly number of surviving Massachusetts sixpence coins (struck 1652-82) and British sixpence of William III (struck 1695-1701) have been bent at one time! There even seems to be a method to this bending: with the obverse facing, the top of the coin is bent back, while the bottom of the coin is bent forward. There are various theories as to why these old sixpence were bent. One particular and popular story holds that a bent sixpence was believed to ward off witches or evil spirits. Moreover, a HOLED and bent silver sixpence allegedly tells us that the coin was worn around the neck of a nervous 17th century citizen for just that purpose. A second theory on bent sixpence, is that they simply brought the owner or wearer good luck. A third theory asserts that bent sixpence were bent in such a way as to be a tool to open snuff boxes. The last theory simply holds that a bent sixpence was easier to find and grab out of one's pocket, not to mention easier to KEEP in one's pocket (a bent coin wouldn't fall through a hole in the pocket so easily)!

SLAVE TAGS: A "slave tag" was oftentimes simply a smoothed-out British copper halfpence that was holed, and an incused number stamped onto the face of it. Sometimes both sides were smoothed out, sometimes just one side. Such slave tags seem to have been most prevalent in the mid-1700's to early 1800's. Many a dealer no doubt has sold such pieces as discounted "junk" (after all, it's super worn AND holed). But don't YOU make the mistake of considering such a piece to be junk. If you see a worn old copper with a big hole, an incused (indented as opposed to raised) number on the face of it.... SWIPE IT UP! There is a strong market for such historical pieces, pieces that undoubtedly tell a sad, tragic tale from our country's earliest days.

COUNTER-MARKED/COUNTER-STAMPED COINS: It would be tempting to say counter-marked or counter-stamped coins are victims of vandalism or graffiti. But back in the olden days, a counter-mark or counter-stamp wasn't necessarily employed to deface a coin in a malicious sense. Counter-marking/counter-stamping coins was a common practice going back to Ancient Greece and continuing up into the early 1900's. Only in more modern times has the practice largely vanished. "Counter-mark" and "Counter-stamp" are very nearly the same thing. A counter-mark is an incused number stamped into the face of a coin. A counter-stamp would be a RAISED strike of an inscription, number or design struck OVER the original design. I've seen the terms 'counter-mark' and 'counter-stamp' often used interchangeably, so don't get too hung up over the semantics. We've already discussed one notable counter-mark, that being an incused slave tag numeral onto the face of an old coin. Below are three samples of commonly-seen Colonial/early American counter-marked and counter-stamped coins:

1. *Caribbean Counter-marks*: Back in the 1700's, worn-out British and French silver coins featured crude numeral counter-marks to specify a new "denomination" for a particular island. For instance, a '9' incused onto the face of a worn silver coin would indicate that the coin would now circulate as a 9 denier coin on the island of Tobago. In addition to numerals, letters might also appear as counter-marks, such as a cursive 'T' (for Trinidad) or 'D' for Domingo.

2. *Central America Republic Counter-Stamps*: In the 1830's to 1850's, a small circular design featuring a mountain range with the sun-rays behind them was often counter-stamped over worn 18th century Spanish silver cob coins.

3. *Advertising Counter-Marks*: A host of such counter-marks appear on the faces of 18th century Spanish-Colonial silver coins, 17th-18th century British copper coins and 18th-19th century U.S. coins. For instance, the name and

address of a New York theater might be incused onto the face of a 1794 Spanish-Colonial two reales. A clothier might stamp the name of his business or business address onto the face of a 1797 U.S. large cent. Know this – any coin with a counter-mark that can be directly linked to a known early American business, institution or person, is a truly valuable piece! The more specific and informative the advertising, the more valuable the coin to collectors. Also be on the lookout for scroll-like counter-stamps with a name inside them. These are known as "silversmith stamps," and were employed onto worn copper coins in the U.S. around the 1820's-40's period.

SLICED SPANISH SILVER: Talk about damage to a coin! It doesn't get any worse than taking a perfectly good coin and chopping it into bits! Then, again... some collectors WANT a ½ or ¼ of a coin in their collection of early American coins! Why? Because it was a common practice in Colonial America to take a milled Spanish or Spanish-Colonial eight reales coin and cut it into smaller denominations– much like the way you'd slice up a pie: slice it in half, and both pieces equal a four reales; slice each half in two and you have four "two reales." Cut each quarter in half, and you have eight "one-real" coins. This was quite a commonly accepted practice in Colonial America due to scarcity of small denomination silver coins. This means that if you ever come across such a sliced piece of Spanish silver, you can bet it likely bounced around the streets of Colonial and/or early America!

1700-46 Spanish 2 Reales "Pistareen"

CHAPTER EIGHTEEN

A COIN OF COLONIAL WILLIAMSBURG

(1700-46 Spanish 'Pistareen')

Colonial Williamsburg is truly unique. To step onto Colonial Williamsburg's main thoroughfare, Duke of Gloucester Street, is to feel transported back to 1774! This thoroughfare may not be dirt or crowded with mules and horse-drawn carriages, but just about everything else has the authentic look and feel of a pre-Revolutionary War town. Georgian-styled clapboard and brick houses, taverns and shops line the streets. "Ghosts" from the past, gentlemen and ladies in Colonial garb, wander the town and chat with 21st century visitors, enlightening them as to life in 1774 Virginia.

Colonial Williamsburg is not just a special place because it's a fully-restored Colonial village. Williamsburg was a very important center in Colonial times, even though it was never a large city like Boston, Philadelphia or New York. Still, Williamsburg was the capital of Virginia from 1699 to

1780, and Virginia was one of the more populated of the Thirteen Colonies. Big names are connected with early Williamsburg. It can boast of such luminaries as George Washington, Thomas Jefferson and Patrick Henry debating Colonial affairs in the capitol building at the end of Duke Of Gloucester Street! Incidentally, Thomas Jefferson also attended law school in Williamsburg, at the College Of William & Mary.

In short, Colonial Williamsburg has Colonial history to spare! And because it was the capital of Virginia during much of America's Colonial period, Williamsburg attracted many visitors. When the House of Burgess was in session, the inns and taverns of Williamsburg were at full capacity. Gentlemen wearing white wigs sat around tavern tables, smoking pipes, swapping stories, debating issues. In such a setting, money often changed hands. Coins. But what were the coins exchanged in Colonial Williamsburg, say, circa 1774?

There were many. Coins from numerous countries circulated on the streets of Williamsburg. There were the silver and gold coins of Spanish-Colonial America. There were British copper halfpennies and farthings. French, Dutch and Portuguese silver and gold coins were not uncommon either. But, judging from the archaeological evidence, one coin in particular can truly be crowned the reigning "Coin Of Colonial Williamsburg." It is not a British halfpenny of George II or George III. It is not even a Spanish-Colonial silver coin, the very staple of Colonial commerce elsewhere in the Thirteen Colonies. No, the winner of the grand prize is – drum-roll please– the Spanish two reales!

Wait a minute– didn't I just contradict myself? Nope. There were the Spanish-Colonial silver coins that circulated in Williamsburg and elsewhere throughout the Colonies. These coins were struck in the Spanish mints of Mexico, Peru, Bolivia, Chile and Guatemala. Then there were the silver coins of SPAIN- struck in the mints of the Spanish mainland. These ALSO circulated throughout the British Colonies. For some reason, it seems more of the Spanish mainland silver coins circulated in Williamsburg, than did the Spanish-Colonial silver coins. The reverse would have been true just about everywhere else in the Thirteen Colonies, but Williamsburg was the exception. Why, I'm not sure.

All right, what else do we know about these Spanish silver coins of Williamsburg? For starters, they are all either one-real or two reales struck under Phillip V, who reigned 1700-46. All the ones found date 1717 to 1736, but that doesn't mean the earlier or later Phillip V dates did not also circulate in Williamsburg. Of the two denominations, it is the two reales coin that has turned up most often, though some of those two reales have been halved or quartered to make smaller change. So, from the evidence found, I think we can safely conclude that our ideal "Coin Of Colonial Williamsburg," would be a 1700-46 Spanish (not Spanish-Colonial) two reales of Phillip V.

The 1700-46 Spanish two reales or "Pistareen," is easily distinguishable from the Spanish-Colonial two reales of roughly the same period, namely the Pillar-Type two reales. The Spanish-Colonial Pillar two reales shows a crowned globe between pillars on the obverse, a crowned shield of arms on the reverse. The Phillip V pistareen has a large cross with the shield of Castile and Leon on one side, a crowned Hapsburg shield on the reverse. Later, In 1772, the Spanish mainland would strike a smaller-sized two reales with a bust of King Charles III on the obverse– in Colonial times, these were known as "head pistareens."

Maybe you've heard that the Spanish two reales is the forerunner of the U.S. quarter. So that means there were TWO different types of Spanish "quarters" or "two-bits" circulating in Colonial Williamsburg– the Spanish and Spanish-Colonial two reales? Not exactly. Here again, we must differentiate between the Spanish-Colonial two reales and its Spanish mainland counterpart. The 1700-46 Spanish pistareens did not contain as much silver as the Spanish-Colonial two reales. Consequently, while it took four Spanish-Colonial two reales to equal a peso, or dollar, it took FIVE pistareens to equal the same amount! So, if the Spanish-Colonial two reales can rightly be considered the true forerunner of the U.S. quarter, then the Spanish pistareen is actually the forerunner of... the U.S. Twenty-Cent coin!

What? The United States actually had a Twenty-Cent coin? Yes. Briefly. They were struck from 1875 to 1878, but only in 1875 were they struck in quantity. The Twenty-Cent piece was highly unpopular with the American public – it looked too much like the current quarter in size and design! But that's another story. What's important is that the United States had an eye to making Twenty-Cent coins long before 1875! In his report to the Continental Congress in 1779, Gouvenor Morris wrote, "we need a pistareen." In 1786, plans for an American coinage included recommendations for "double-dimes" or pistareens. It didn't actually happen, but it does show how important the pistareen was in 18th century America!

As recently as the late 1990's, I often found 1700-46 Spanish pistareens in average circulated condition for around $5- $10, however, it's getting harder and harder to find them at such low prices. They're good-sized silver coins from the early 1700's, and with that large Spanish cross on the obverse, they have that "pirate coin" look to them. Hence, the bidding seems to be pretty lively for these coins on eBay. A better bet might be to visit a large coin show where there are dealers who specialize in old world coins (boy, is THAT mantra going to be repeated often in this book). Every so often "problem" pistareens pop up in dealer junk boxes for just a few dollars apiece. Such "problem" pistareens may have a hole or two, smudging in the legend and date area or slight bends. And since the 1700-46 pistareen doesn't have a high catalogue value, VOILA, into the junk box goes the problem pistareen. That's when you swoop in.

Even if you can't pick up a cheap pistareen in a dealer junk box, it's probably still possible, with some looking, to pick up a low to average circulated Phillip V pistareen on eBay for $15-$25. Especially if it has some of the aforementioned problems. Add this coin to your collection! George Washington handled these as a boy and as a young man. It's time to hold this historic piece of Colonial Williamsburg in your hands too!

1719-25 French Copper Sol of Louis XV

CHAPTER NINETEEN

COINS OF EARLY FRENCH NEW ORLEANS

(1719-25 French "John Law" Coppers)

Though the first French settlement in the Louisiana territory was the fort at Biloxi in 1699, a new settlement at the mouth of the Mississippi River would become the capital of the Louisiana Colony. Governor Bienville founded New Orleans here in November of 1718. There were only 68 settlers at first, but Bienville had high hopes for his new settlement.

Indeed, New Orleans began to grow. By December of 1719, German farmers arrived in the area, fleeing the wars of Louis XIV and seeking to settle on land they could call their own.Since the first settlers of New Orleans had been French convicts, the industrious German farmers were welcomed by the founder of the Company of the West, John Law. More about John Law a little later.

Early on there was a serious shortage of women in the gulf coast area, but this problem was resolved in 1721 when a shipload of French women arrived at Ship Island near Biloxi. These were not exactly women of high society; in fact, many came from houses of correction in France. Some were prostitutes, and some were orphans in their early teens. Nevertheless, they were welcomed enthusiastically by the men of Louisiana, many of whom eagerly paddled out to the island to greet them! Some of the newly-arrived women were married in Biloxi shortly after setting foot on New World soil! The others scattered to the French settlements of Biloxi, Mobile and New Orleans where they too, found eager husbands.

Governor Bienville was not thrilled at what he saw transpiring. Louisiana was already populated by male murderers, thieves and other convicts, many who came to the New World in chains! Now, female convicts, prostitutes and orphans were added to the mix! But then, Bienville himself had petitioned John Law (more on him later!) many times for women to be shipped to the colony, particularly for the restless Canadian soldiers stationed there. In one letter, Bienville wrote, " Send me wives for my Canadians. They are running into the woods after Indian girls. "

Thus did New Orleans get its start. The settlement grew over time, eventually becoming the chief French port of the Louisiana territory. The city came under the control of Spain in 1762, but was again returned to French rule in 1800. Finally, in 1803, New Orleans and all the Louisiana territory was purchased by the United States. During that time, New Orleans had become a mix of New World and Old World cultures. In addition to the early French and German settlers, New Orleans also hosted Spanish, British, Yankee, American Indian and African West Indies cultures. Not only did these cultures mix together, but they did so relatively isolated from the rest of the population centers of America's east coast. Consequently, a uniquely southern/Louisiana/New Orleans-culture developed, making New Orleans almost a world unto itself, exotically different from other American cities.

So what would constitute a collectible early New Orleans coin? An easy answer would be, any copper or silver French coin from the reigns of Louis XIV or Louis XV. But we can get more specific than that. Certainly a good choice would be the French Colonial copper sou (or nine deniers) coins of 1721 and 1722. Some 500,000 of these coins were actually shipped to New Orleans from France, but they were poorly received. An edict from Louis XV in 1726 attempted to force the acceptance of these coppers, but in the end, all but about 8,000 of these coins were returned to France. These sous of 1721 and 1722 can be found in today's marketplace, but are pretty scarce, and will cost about $65-$85 for even a some-what less than average circulated piece. I think there is a very attractive, and much less costly, alternative.

Remember that John Law fellow I mentioned earlier? Here's how HE fits into the story of early New Orleans AND early New Orleans coinage. In 1717, the Regent of France met up with Scotsman and financier, John Law. Law somehow convinced the Regent, Philip of Orleans, to give Law's company, Company of the West, control of the Louisiana territory. Law had the grand idea of populating the Louisiana territory with white settlers. Those settlers would exploit the region's gold, silver and diamond resources. Eager investors jumped at the investment opportunity to pluck their money down and (hopefully) get rich! The project was dubbed, "Le Mississippi." Today, it's referred to as the "Mississippi Bubble."

By October of 1720, the bubble burst for Law and his investors. New Orleans had been established, but little gold, silver or diamonds was discovered in the crude, shanty-filled New Orleans area or the humid, jungle-like Mississippi Valley region. John Law had issued thousands of shares of overpriced stock to finance "Le Mississippi," but the stock crashed. Investors saw their dreams of riches turn to dust, and Law was forced to step down as head of the Company of the West. By 1731, Company of the West's trade rights had passed back to the French crown.

That brings us to a coinage series known as "John Law" coppers. These coins were not struck under the authority of John Law, but they were struck in France during the period of roughly 1719-21 when John Law and his company held sway over the Louisiana territory. Actually, the copper liards, half-sols and sols were struck from 1719 to 1725. The 1720 issues are especially linked to John Law and the "Mississippi Bubble." In fact, the *Red Book* even lists the 1720 France sol, though it does not list the smaller liards and half-sols.

Granted there will always be a dispute as to whether these "John Law" copper coins, or even other specific "French Colonial" coins, should rightfully be considered "American Colonials." Why? Because there is always disagreement as to which French and French-Colonial coins were meant to circulate in France, in the French Indies, in Canada or in the Louisiana Territory. My advice: don't worry about it. If you happen to find an affordable "John Law" liard or sol, grab it!

The "John Law" coppers are actually official coins of France that feature a bust of young Louis XV (not John Law) on the obverse and a crowned shield of arms, surrounded by legend, on the reverse. They are most certainly coins that could (and almost certainly DID) come over to New Orleans back in its early, 1720's shanty-town state. The same would hold true for the coins dated 1722-25, even though those dated 1719-21 would have the stronger John Law connection.

"John Law" coppers are often sold simply as French coins, making it possible for you to get one at an affordable price. For example, I won a 1724 French liard (and it was offered as simply that) on eBay recently, for $4.50! If you want to find one of these pieces on eBay, simply go to the Coins section and type in such keywords as "172* France," "172* French" or "John Law." Believe it or not, recent world coin catalogues list these 1719-1725 liards and sols of France at retail prices of $5-$15 in average circulated condition! In my opinion, they are highly under-valued!

1749 British Halfpenny of George II

CHAPTER TWENTY

COINS THAT SAILED
TO BOSTON IN 1749

(1749 British Halfpence & Farthings)

A good many copper George II halfpence (and to a lesser extent, farthings) circulated in Colonial America. This is a fairly well-known fact to virtually anyone with a general knowledge of Colonial coins. What is not as well known is that one date in particular stands out above the others when it comes to George II coppers. That would be the 1749-dated farthings and halfpence.

Prior to 1749, there were indeed copper coins circulating in the Colonies. Halfpennies and farthings of William III, George I and George II certainly made the rounds in such population centers as New York, Boston and Philadelphia. But more copper coinage was needed. Paper money was also prevalent, but merchants wanted hard money. Finally, in September of 1749, the British vessel *The Mermaid* arrived in Boston. Aboard this vessel was a large shipment of British copper coins, along with some Spanish silver coins. These coins were sent to the Colonies courtesy of British parliament, as payment to the Massachusetts Bay Colony for their aid in an early French and Indian War conflict.

It was a significant influx of copper: some 800,000 halfpence and more than 420,000 farthings!All dated 1749! In fact, this shipment of copper coins was so large and unanticipated, the Massachusetts authorities had a difficult time finding a suitable place to safely store them! In time, however, the welcome coppers filtered out into circulation. They passed from hand to hand throughout the Thirteen Colonies. They found their way to large seaport cities, southern plantation towns and forest-surrounded villages. Colonists used them to buy bread, drink, shoes, pipes and tobacco, a room at the inn, books, feed for livestock and perhaps even a wig (for the men, as well as the women).

And what was going on in the Colonies in 1749 and the years following? We've already learned that all those 1749 coppers were payment for the colonists aid in a conflict with France. That conflict, however, was not the official "French and Indian War." Actually, there had been a series of New World battles between the British and French, dating back to the late 1600's. From that time to the mid-1700's, Great Britain and France were at continual odds with each other over North American supremacy. Both Great Britain and France sought out the Native American tribes as allies, but Britain had the advantage in that the colonists would also fight alongside the British regulars against France.

The BIG and most famous conflict, of course, was the French and Indian War of 1753-60. Fought mostly in New York and into Canada, this long and bloody struggle at last saw France ousted as a major Colonial power in North America. If you've ever read the classic book, Last Of The Mohicans (or saw the smash hit 1992 movie version), then you at least have a picture of this period. And it is precisely during those unsettled years that the 1749 copper halfpence and farthings were circulating!

What does all this mean to the collector of Colonial and early American coins? It means that while any George II halfpence or farthing is a worthy remnant of our heritage, a 1749-dated halfpence or farthing is a *crucial* remnant of our Colonial heritage! Any 1749-dated British copper stands an excellent chance of having been aboard *The Mermaid* when it sailed into the port of Boston. As such, that coin almost definitely saw Colonial circulation.

As of this writing, price guides for 18th century British coins do not price 1749 halfpennies or farthings any higher than other dates from George II's reign! Use that to your advantage while you can! As with other coins discussed in this book, it is not general knowledge yet that 1749 British coppers have a strong Colonial connection! Occasionally you will see a 1749 halfpence or farthing listed on eBay, detailing the coin's possible link to that 1749 shipment. But I have seen many other listings that do NOT detail the story behind these 1749-dated coppers– they are sold without fanfare as 1749 halfpennies or farthings.

But now *you* know better! Folks, this is one British coin that deserves a LOT of fanfare!

1720 British Halfpenny of George I

CHAPTER TWENTY-ONE

EVEN BETTER THAN A "1776" COIN!

(1717-24 British Halfpenny Of George I)

Wouldn't it be great to own a coin that was present at the signing of the Declaration Of Independence in 1776? Well, we don't know what coins were actually in the room when that famous document was ratified and signed by such luminaries as John Hancock, Samuel Adams, Benjamin Franklin and Thomas Jefferson! It would seem only logical to assume that one or more of the signers of the Declaration had a few coins in his pocket on that historic day in 1776. The problem is, we don't know for SURE what coins were there at the signing of the Declaration Of Independence — how could one ever know that without the use of a time machine?

We DO know, however, of one specific coin that was there. While this particular coin was not inside the assembly hall, it WAS on the grounds of Independence Hall at the very moment of the signing. The coin in question? A 1717-24 British halfpence of George I.

The 270 year-old copper coin was found in 1996 by an archaeologist excavating beneath the grand staircase leading into Independence Hall. The archaeologist, Paul Inashimas, was digging a trench inside the west wall of the tower for the purpose of examining the foundation of the historic Philadelphia building. The tower was built in the 1750's, and Inashimas believes a Colonial workman lost the coin at that time. There it lay, beneath the grand staircase, as nearly thirty more years of Colonial history marched by, while outside the walls of Independence Hall the Colonies were embroiled in the French and Indian War from 1753-60. There it lay, through the 1760's, as the colonists grew more and more disenchanted with the taxes and restrictions imposed on them by the British crown; through the early 1770's as tumultuous events and tensions outside the walls of Independence Hall were moving the Colonies to a break with the Mother Country.

What if coins had the ability to hear? Well, if they could, then one day in July of 1776, our humble George I halfpenny heard the throaty shouts of a large gathering of legislators. Perhaps our halfpenny heard someone declare loudly, "Resolution passed, " followed by loud cheers and shouts of "Independence! Independence! " Eventually, the shouting and din died down, and all was quiet again in the unending darkness of the spot in Independence Hall where the halfpenny lay.

For the next five years, the harsh and bloody Revolutionary War was fought in the countryside outside Independence Hall and Philadelphia. In the winter of 1778, as our George I halfpenny lay in the chilly darkness of Independence Hall, just a few miles away, General George Washington and the Continental Army were suffering in their encampment at Valley Forge. And surely, in 1781, our humble George I halfpenny heard the rejoicing of the Philadelphia citizens as news arrived of the British surrender to Washington's army at Yorktown, Virginia.

Time continued to march on. The Unites States of America was now established with George Washington as our first President. The U.S. Mint was established in the city of Philadelphia, thus beginning an era in which official U.S. coins would now take the place of British coins like our George I halfpenny. At the same time, in the 1790's, yellow fever plagued the city of Philadelphia during the summer months, causing widespread evacuation of the city until winter arrived.

Quietly and patiently, our George I copper lay in the darkness of Independence Hall as the United States entered the 1800's. Soldiers would again march outside the walls of Independence Hall– in 1812, and then again in 1861. What began on July 4, 1776, was nearly undone in the years of 1861-65 as the bloody Civil War nearly tore the country apart. Miraculously, the Union survived not only that terrible four-year conflict, but also the assassination of the President who had guided our country through that war. Our George I halfpenny lay undisturbed through it all.

Then came the 20th century. Our nation endured two World Wars, a stock market crash and The Great Depression. Our George I halfpenny must have heard the stirring of the Roaring 20's, the birth of Rock and Roll, the Vietnam conflict and accompanying protests. Then, in 1996, our George I halfpenny hears loud clanging and chipping sounds. At last, a burst of sunlight– the first to bathe our George I halfpenny in nearly 240 years! A pair of hands reach down and pull the sleeping copper coin from the spot where it has rested since the 1750's. If only our Independence Hall George I halfpenny could tell the world what it had seen and heard during those many years!

Obviously, you cannot own that very same George I half-pence that slept – or perhaps lay wide awake, if your imagination prefers– in Independence Hall! But you can own a sibling! George I halfpennies were only struck for a few years, 1717-24. They were, however, struck in large enough numbers that tracking down a specimen is not too difficult. Once more, the news is good: a low to average circulated piece should cost only $8-$18. More good news is that these George I halfpennies were struck in higher relief than later British halfpence of George II and George III, thus it's much easier to see the design, even on worn examples.

If you can find one, consider my favorite, the 1718 date. That's the year the notorious pirate, Blackbeard was slain off the coast of North Carolina during a ferocious sword fight with Lieutenant Robert Maynard of the Royal Navy. The 1718 halfpence is no more expensive than any of the other dates– in fact, all dates of the George I halfpence series retail about the same.

Incidentally, 1723 is also an interesting date to collect. During that year, there were no less than THREE different 1723 George I copper coins (one was brass, but it looked like copper) of roughly halfpence size, circulating in the American Colonies! There was, of course, the British halfpence of George I. Then there was the 1722-24 Rosa American 2 pence token coins which were basically the same size as the British halfpence. Finally, there were the 1723-24 Hibernia halfpence, which was originally struck for use in Ireland, but being rejected there, it was eventually dumped on the American Colonies. The early 1720's must have been a terribly confusing time in the markets of Colonial America!

1776 Spanish-Colonial 1 Reale of Charles III

CHAPTER TWENTY-TWO

OWN A GENUINE
1776 COLONIAL COIN!

If you find American history AND old coins interesting, then of COURSE you're going to want to own a genuine Colonial coin dated 1776! Is any other date more symbolic of Colonial America? Of our nation's struggle for independence? The year 1776 immediately conjures up mental pictures of Thomas Jefferson, George Washington, Benjamin Franklin and various other Founding Fathers! But where to find an American Colonial coin dated 1776, that's the dilemma.

Search the "Colonial" section of any U.S. coin guide book, and you'll see that there were various American-made coins struck in 1776. You will also notice that these coins are very rare and expensive! You might be able to get your hands on one if you look long and hard...and are willing to mortgage the family farm.

How about a British copper coin? After all, British coppers circulated in the Colonies. Well, yes, there are British halfpennies of George III dated 1776 out there on the market. Mind you, they are counterfeits, but that in itself is not really the problem. The problem is, the majority of

1776-dated counterfeit halfpennies can be traced to 1780's manufacture! All right, enough of the bad news.

The good news is, you CAN own a coin dated 1776. With this coin, not only can the date be trusted, but there is also an excellent chance that very coin circulated in Colonial and/or early America! In fact, this coin was THE primary circulating silver coin of 1776 America! Ready for more good news? This coin is available and affordable! The coin or coins I'm referring to are the Spanish-Colonial silver half real, one real, and two reales.

Struck in the mints of Mexico, Peru, Bolivia, Chile, and Guatemala, the Spanish-Colonial silver coins saw extensive circulation in the Thirteen Colonies, Confederation-Era America, and the early 19th century United States. So common were Spanish-Colonial silver coins in the money markets of America, that our own silver coinage was based largely on the Spanish-Colonial eight reales and its subdivisions. In fact, you could say that the half-real was the was the forerunner of the U.S. half dime; the one real was the forerunner of the U.S. dime; the two reales was the forerunner of the U.S. quarter; the four reale was the forerunner of the U.S. half dollar; and the eight reales, the forerunner of the U.S. silver dollar.

As for the 1776-dated pieces, your best and most affordable bets are the ½, 1 and 2 reales coins. All three denominations are priced roughly the same. As of this writing, it's still possible to acquire a low circulated 1776 piece at $10-$15, an average circulated piece (perhaps with a minor problem or two) for $15-$35. If you want to go for the big 1776 eight reales piece, be prepared to shell out around $75-$100 for an average circulated coin. These prices are very much in flux!

I almost hesitate to list prices because there is often a glaring discrepancy between "catalogue" prices of 1776 Spanish-Colonial silver coins, and the prices I see these coins bring on internet auctions. For instance, recent price guides indicate a retail value of around $45 for an average circulated 1776 Spanish-Colonial eight reales. But I don't think a $45 bid is going to cut the mustard if you're trying to win an average circulated 1776 eight reales on eBay. Amazingly, recent price guides show 1776 Spanish-Colonial silver coins of all denominations, to retail at about the same price levels as other dates in the Charles III silver series (1772-89). That does not correspond with the reality I see. The 1776 Spanish-Colonial two reales may be just as common as, say, a 1773- dated Spanish-Colonial two reales, but guess which coin is going to attract heavier bidding on eBay (all things being equal)?

Still, despite how many collectors battle over 1776-dated Spanish-Colonial silver coins on internet auctions, your saving grace, being a collector on a budget, is this: many coin dealers still price their coins according to retail prices taken from price guides. And remember what I said about 1776-dated Spanish silver still being priced the same as other dates! A few years from now, we may look back and realize how laughably low today's prices are for these 1776 coins! In other words, this is one case where you WANT to pay retail! Sure, try your luck on eBay, but, in my opinion, your best bet is a dealer who sticks to the price guides.

(from top going clockwise)
1827 Mexico 2 Reales, 1808 Mexico 8 Reales of Ferdinand VII, 1823 Mexico ½ Reale of Augustine Iturbide, 1817 Peru 4 Reales of Ferdinand VII

Chapter Twenty-Three

COINS OF THE
CALIFORNIA MISSIONS

If you visit the museum at Mission San Carlos Borromeo de
Carmelo, otherwise known as the Carmel Mission, you'll
find among the displayed artifacts a grouping of excavated
coins. The coins are all silver and almost all are Spanish-
Colonial, along with a few coins of post-Spanish Mexico.
Dates range from the 1770's to around the 1840's. Probably
more coins reached the Carmel Mission than other missions
as this was the headquarters of the entire Alta California
mission network. Important visitors to Alta California, back
in the days of the Spanish missions, were often received and
given lodging at this important mission, located near the
picturesque Carmel Bay.

Coins were not a huge part of mission life itself, since
missions were meant to be self-sustaining. The clothes you
wore, the furniture you sat or slept on, were made on site.
The food you ate was grown on mission farms. Certainly
the mission priests were not laden with coins, as they were
required to take a vow of poverty. Still, as proved by the

151

display at the Carmel Mission Harry Downie Museum, coins still found their way to the missions.

The story of the California missions began in the 1760's. At that time, Spain was increasingly concerned over the Russian presence on the Pacific coast of North America. To protect their interests in that part of the New World, King Charles III of Spain and Jose de Galvez, Visitador-General of New Spain, charged Captain Gasper de Portola with leading an expedition to establish a land route from Baja, California to the Bay of Monterey. Captain Sebastian Vizcaino had described the bay in glowing terms when he explored there in 1602. At the same time, Father Junipero Serra was to accompany Gasper de Portola from Mexico, for the purpose of establishing missions in Alta California. Father Serra was eager for the opportunity.

Serra, a man of diminutive stature at 5'2, was nonetheless a man of gigantic faith, love and determination. A hugely talented administrator, preacher and genius in Christian theology, Father Serra could easily have chosen to serve out his ministry in the far greater comforts of Spain or Spanish Mexico, where a theologian of his ability would always have a place. Instead, Serra could not be dissuaded that his calling was to bring the gospel of Christianity to the natives of Alta California – a land where there were no European cities and none of the comforts he enjoyed growing up in Spain – and to live amongst them for the remainder of his life. In fact, Serra had visions of being martyred in Alta (meaning "upper") California!

In March of 1769, some 300 men accompanied Portola and Serra as they journeyed north from Baja. By the time they reached the bay at San Diego, more than half of the men had died! Here, the expedition split up. Portola took the able-bodied men and continued north, hoping to rendezvous with a supply ship at Monterey Bay. Serra remained behind with the sick members of the expedition. During his stay in San

Diego, Serra founded the first of the California missions, San Diego de Alcala.

Meanwhile, Portola was experiencing what could only be called a comedy-of-errors were there not so much suffering involved. When he and his men arrived at Monterey Bay, they didn't recognize it, and there was no sign of a supply ship. Deciding they had not yet reached the fabled Bay of Monterey, the expedition proceeded on northward. It was an agonizingly slow march as the men fought scurvy, diarrhea, horrific rainstorms and cold weather. At last, they reached the San Francisco Bay. As fabulous as this discovery was, Portola and his men were still discouraged, since there was no supply ship waiting for them there.

The Portola expedition ended up marching BACK the 500 miles to San Diego. There, Portola and Serra discussed what had transpired, finally agreeing that Portola actually HAD found the Bay of Monterey! It took some persuading, but Serra finally convinced Portola to take yet another trip north. This time, Serra would sail north on a supply ship, and would rendezvous with Portola at Monterey Bay.

Finally, success. Portola arrived at Monterey Bay on May 23, 1770. A week later, the *San Antonio* arrived by sea, bearing both supplies and Father Junipero Serra. On June 3, 1770, Father Serra and the men of the Portola expedition celebrated mass at the water's edge. Cannons were fired (scaring away curious native onlookers) and Monterey Bay was once again claimed for Spain.

Immediately, a crude presidio was constructed only yards from the bay, since the immediate danger in Portola's mind, was an attack by the Russians! Such an attack never materialized. A temporary church was built within the walls of the presidio. Serra and the Franciscans under his authority, began trying to convert the local Rumsen and Ohlone Indians.

Portola did not stay long since he had little affection for Alta California. In fact, he was to confide to a friend in a letter, "If the Russians want Alta California, they should have it." Portola felt that Alta California was so isolated that any attempt to supply provisions or military aid was far too costly, time-consuming and dangerous. The priests and friars may have welcomed the hardship, but to a non-cleric European, California was the uncivilized edge of the world! It was a land of wild animals, harsh wilderness, and desolation, a land without cities, a land seldom visited by ships.

Despite their location at the "edge of the world," the Spanish presidio of Monterey survived. It wasn't long, however, before Father Serra and his friars decided to move their mission away from the presidio of Monterey. Evidently, the Spanish soldiers were behaving in an unseemly manner with the native women Serra hoped to convert to Christianity! Thus, in 1771, Mission San Carlos Borromeo de Carmelo was founded near the mouth of the Carmel River, just over the hill from Monterey.

Father Serra was not content with having founded the two missions at San Diego and Carmel Bay. He began establishing other mission sites up and down the coast (or I should say, NEAR the coast, since few of the missions sat right next to the ocean). In all, Serra founded nine missions in Alta California before he died in 1784 of natural causes. Serra, whom many consider to be the founder and Father of California, died in his humble, sparsely-furnished cell at the Mission San Carlos. Apparently, God didn't approve of his vision of martyrdom. He was a man who, by all accounts, truly loved the people he served, and was loved in return.

Eventually, 21 Franciscan missions would be established in California, the last being St. Francis of Solano, located near San Francisco, in 1823. Most of the missions were set up along the south-north road called the El Camino Reale, first blazed by Gasper de Portola in 1769. The mission sites were chosen so that each mission would be no more than a day's journey apart on the El Camino Reale.

Certainly there is some controversy regarding the legacy of the Spanish missions in California. The neophyte Indians at the missions were not exactly free to come and go as they pleased. Spanish soldiers often rode out to round up runaways and bring them back to the missions by force. Also, not all of the Spanish friars who served in the missions were Serra's equal in the areas of kindess and compassion. Consequently, in early 1800's, there were scattered native revolts, particularly down near Santa Barbara. Still, it can be argued that the missions prevented greater violence against the natives of California. Remember that from the 1770's through the 1820's, the European presence in Alta California consisted mostly of Spanish missions or Spanish forts. Had it not been for the influence of the priests and the missions, the California Indians would have been left almost completely at the mercy of a more secular-minded populace whose concern for the physical and spiritual welfare of the natives would have been minimal. We see this in the behavior of some of the Spanish soldiers, particularly in their dealings with native women. The California Native Americans were to later to suffer far greater violence at the hands of Yankee treasure-seekers during the Gold Rush years.

The power and influence of the missions were in significant decline by 1822, when news of Mexico's independence from Spain reached upper California. Though the Franciscan friars voted to give their allegiance to the new government of Mexico, the friars' days were numbered. In 1834, the Mexican governor of Alta California declared that mission lands would be divided between the Indians and the Californios (settlers of Spanish-Mexican descent). With the secularization of the mission lands, the hey-day of California missions came to an end. Most of the Spanish missions had fallen into ruin by the late 1800's, but were resurrected in the 20th century as churches and historical attractions.

For around $15 each, you can build a nice little three-coin "California Missions Coin Set." Below is my choice–certainly other groupings are possible. Such coins are regularly available on eBay (under the "Coins" categories of Colonials, Mexico, Peru, Bolivia) and also at large coins shows, particularly West Coast coin shows.

1789-1809 Spanish-Colonial ½ Real:
$8-$15 in average circulated condition

1809-21 Spanish-Colonial 1 Real:
$8-$15 in average circulated condition

1825-34 Mexico 2 Reales:
$12-$20 in average circulated condition

1783 Spanish-Colonial 8 Reales
from El Cazador Shipwreck

CHAPTER TWENTY-FOUR

DID THESE COINS CHANGE THE COURSE OF NORTH AMERICAN HISTORY?

(Spanish-Colonial Silver Coins Of 1784 El Cazador Shipwreck)

I t's not often you can point to a particular coin and say, "This coin could have changed the course of history!" Yet, if you're holding one of the Spanish silver coins from the 1784 shipwreck of the El Cazador, you can! Mind you, these coins didn't actually change the course of American history by what they did, but by what they DIDN'T do. Simply put, they didn't arrive.

It's the early 1780's, and America's Louisiana territory (think present-day Louisiana, Arkansas, Texas, and up into Missouri) is Spanish territory. The economic situation in Spanish Louisiana is not good. The smattering of Spanish, French and Yankee settlers don't have enough hard money to go around. Instead, the money in circulation consists mostly of Spanish paper currency, deemed largely worthless by the local populace.

Finally, King Charles III of Spain decides the time has come to stabilize the monetary system of his North American holdings. Charles III authorizes a huge shipment of Spanish silver coins, struck in Mexico City, to be sent from Mexico to New Orleans. This shipment consists of 450,000 pesos, most of that being in the form of large Spanish-Colonial eight reales, known the world over for their high-quality silver content. Smaller denominations of Spanish silver coin are also part of this shipment.

On January 11, 1784, a Spanish man-o-war brigantine, the El Cazador, sets sail from Vera Cruz, Mexico, bound for New Orleans. On board the El Cazador is the huge cargo of newly-minted Spanish-Colonial silver coinage. Of course, the Colonial authorities and settlers of the Louisiana Territory eagerly await the shipment. There will be little wasted time in releasing these high-quality coins into circulation, and the sooner these coins spread out over the Spanish Louisiana Territory, the sooner the hated Spanish paper currency will be driven out! The sooner the Spanish paper currency is driven from circulation, the sooner Spanish North America can become a stable and prosperous financial territory for Spain!

But that never happens because the El Cazador never reaches the port of New Orleans. Spanish Colonial authorities in Louisiana can only assume the ship ran into one of the notorious winter storms and went down to Davy Jones Locker. This is another crushing economic blow to Spain whose coffers are already almost empty from nearly 300 years of wars, Colonial exploration, and expansion! With the loss of El Cazador's cargo, Spain's North American holdings grow ever weaker.

What to do? Well, Spain decides it's time to start the ball rolling on either selling or trading away her Louisiana territories. The year is 1800, and King Charles IV hands Louisiana back over to France (who actually owned the Louisiana Territory BEFORE Spain) for some minor European concessions. France doesn't hold onto it for very long. Emperor Napoleon of France is in need of some extra cash himself, so he ends up selling Louisiana to the United States! Remember, at this time we are talking about a huge chunk of the present-day United States, not just today's state of Louisiana! The purchase price: 15 million dollars. That works out to around three cents an acre! Thomas Jefferson gets himself a deal and a half, to say the least! Doesn't this tale read a lot like one of Paul Harvey's "Now you know the REST of the story?"

So, what if that huge cargo of Spanish silver coins HAD reached New Orleans in 1784? It's highly possible that the coins WOULD have stabilized Spanish North America. If so, odds are that Spain would NOT have sold Louisiana to France. If that had been the case, would that have meant the United States would never have expanded west of the Mississippi? Or would the United States have gone to war with Spain to win the west? Might it have come to that? It's fascinating to speculate just what might have happened had those silver coins on board the El Cazador reached their destination! The history of this country might have been very different!

However, the story of the lost coins of the El Cazador doesn't end there! Many of these coins HAVE reached our shores, but not as circulating coins. They're here now as collectible pieces of history from the shipwreck that just might have been responsible for 1803's Louisiana Purchase! What's more, YOU can own a coin from this famous shipwreck! Recovered in 1993, they are still available at reasonable prices in all levels of preservation and often turn up on eBay..

What can you expect to pay for an El Cazador shipwreck coin ? Well-preserved pieces, especially the eight reales, will cost you anywhere from about $80 to $200. However, there are a number of sea-corroded (but identifiable) El Cazador coins that can be purchased on eBay and at El Cazador coin web sites, for anywhere from $15 to $45 (especially the denominations lower than the eight reales). El Cazador coins are all dated 1783 (at least all that I have seen). Right now, prices are quite reasonable for coins of this historical magnitude, so going for one now might be a good strategy. As one old saying goes, a GOOD strategy today is better than a GREAT strategy tomorrow!

c. 750-1000 A.D Islamic Silver Dirham

CHAPTER TWENTY-FIVE

A VIKING COIN
OF NORTH AMERICA?

(750-1000 A.D Islamic Silver Dirham)

S omeday, someone digging in the soil of the northern
United States or Canada might be puzzled to unearth
a silver coin that is over 1,000 years old. Why? Because
an expert will examine the coin and determine that it's an
Islamic silver dirham struck in Baghdad or some other
Arabian city, sometime between 800 A.D. and 1000 A.D.
Such a discovery would seem to fly in the face of everything
we know about early American history. But I believe such a
scenario is entirely possible, maybe even likely. That's why
we're going to discuss a type of coin very possibly brought
over by North America's earliest coin-using settlers. A coin
you yourself can easily own!

Of course, we now know that Columbus and the Spanish
were not the first Europeans to "discover" the New World.
A band of blonde and red-haired people sailed from Europe
to America some 500 years before Columbus, but unlike

Columbus, these hardy explorers and settlers kept news of their discovery mostly to themselves. Consequently, Columbus, who recorded his trip, gets credit for "discovering" the New World. Still, there is enough documentation and archaeological evidence to credit these "Dark Age" explorers as the first Europeans to land on American shores. Who were these people? They came from the region of northern Europe that is today comprised of Sweden, Denmark and Norway. In olden times they were known as the "Norsemen." Today, they are more commonly known as the Vikings.

My first exposure to Vikings occurred when I was less than five years old. There was a 1967 television series about Vikings, and my most vivid recollection of the show is a scene in which a Viking warrior blows into a horn, then cries out "Vi-KINGS!" Much fighting and mayhem ensued. So from what I saw on that TV show, Vikings were pretty scary customers, with their dragon-headed ships, horned helmets, and thirst for battle and pillage.

Hollywood aside, the Vikings of history truly were pretty scary customers, especially if your village or city was on the receiving end of one of their raids! In fact, an oft-repeated prayer uttered in the British Isles during the Viking Age went, "From the fury of the Northmen, deliver us, Oh Lord." In other words, if you lived in England, Ireland or France, it struck terror in your heart to see you had visitors from the north arriving in dragon-headed ships.

The Viking Age dawned in 793 A.D. when Norsemen warriors set sail from the frigid regions of northern Europe. Their aim was not simply to wreak havoc, but to ease the overcrowding situation in their homeland. Conquering and settling the farm lands to the south was good way to accomplish this, so they sailed to Ireland. First, they raided the Irish monasteries, plundered their treasures and savagely killed the monks. The terrified monks had never seen the likes of these tall, fierce, red-bearded pagan warriors. In fact, one monk who attempted to greet the raiders was met with an axe to the face!

This was just the beginning of the violence that continued for more than two centuries as the Vikings raided the British Isles, France, Eastern Europe, and even as far as the mighty Byzantium Empire (which they failed to conquer). However, it was not all pillage and carnage with the Vikings. Once they had conquered a locale and established their rule, they often administered the area well, and dealt fairly with the local populace. The Vikings, in addition to being fierce warriors, were also able farmers and traders. In time, many of the Vikings turned from their warrior-gods and actually converted to Christianity.

Around 1000 A.D., a band of Vikings, led by Leif Ericson, set sail across the sea to the west, looking for new lands to settle. At last they arrived in what they deemed "Vinland," but today we know it as North America– more specifically, Canada. The Norsemen established the tiny settlement of L'Anse aux Meadows just off the coast of Newfoundland where they stayed just a few years. The settlement didn't prosper– the land was not good for farming and conflicts with the local natives made life even more difficult. So they left. Their stay in Vinland was rather uneventful, but inquiring minds want to know. "did the Vikings bring over any coins with them? " Well, we know of at least one specific coin that almost certainly came over with the Vikings.

That the Vikings must have brought at least a few coins to the New World is proved by the discovery of the "Maine Penny," actually a silver penny of Norway, struck between 1065 and 1080 (yes, pennies existed 1,000 years ago)! It was found in 1957 at an old Native American site off the coast of Maine. The site dates back to around 1200. Those of you who have done a little reading about the Viking settlement in North America may be puzzled at this point. For starters, what is a Viking-era coin doing all the way down in the northern United States? Isn't it generally accepted that the Viking's small settlement was at L'Anse aux Meadows up in Newfoundland? And wouldn't this 1065-80 coin actually date some fifty years AFTER the Norsemen settlers left North America?

Though some experts have their questions about the Maine Penny, most scholars acknowledge that it is indeed a North American Viking artifact. True, it dates some fifty years after the L'Anse aux Meadows settlers are believed to have abandoned Vinland. Still, it's absolutely plausible that the Vikings continued to visit Vinland after the settlement ended for the purpose of hunting and fishing. It is believed the Maine Penny probably came over on one of these later Viking voyages. And how did it come to be found at an old Native American site in Maine? One theory is that the Viking fishermen/hunters ventured south and traded with the natives of that region, but the more accepted theory is that the old village site, located on the coast near Penobscot, Maine, was a Native American trading hub. Perhaps the Viking silver penny was brought down to Maine in the 11th century by natives of Newfoundland trading with the tribesmen of Maine.

Well, that is all well and good and quite interesting, and if you can find a 1065-80 Norwegian penny of Olaf Kyrre, congratulations, as they are rare and quite costly. However, there are other more affordable Viking coins, such as the silver English pennies struck under the Viking ruler, Canute, in the years 1016-35. But even the silver pennies of Canute are not easy to obtain and will start around $150 even in average circulated condition. There is a much more affordable, much easier to obtain "Viking" coin that you can own. It is this coin, I believe, that could still someday be found on North American soil: the Islamic silver dirham of 754-1000 A.D.

We've already mentioned that the Vikings were enthusiastic traders as well as raiders. They ventured as far south as the Mediterranean Sea, and in doing so, encountered the

Arab world. Unlike Western Europe in 793-1000 A.D., the Arab civilizations were NOT experiencing the "Dark Ages." In fact, in the Islamic world, there were strong, established cities, central leadership and an advanced culture. In other words, the Vikings could not sweep into Arab nations and conquer them as easily as they did the less developed countries of Western Europe. Therefore, the Vikings were content to settle for a trading relationship with the Arabs.

The Arabs had an ample supply of one commodity the Vikings truly coveted– silver. So the Vikings initiated a vigorous trade relationship with Arab nations. As a result, Viking treasure hoards generally overflow with silver, much of it in the form of silver coins. That's why a typical Viking burial or "treasure hoard" often consists of Islamic silver dirhams and the huge multiple silver dirhams. It is small wonder the Vikings favored Islamic silver coins. They were made of good silver and were also larger and sturdier than the standard silver coin of Western Europe, the silver penny. In addition, Islamic silver coins were struck in large numbers.

The same silver coin collected by the mighty Vikings can be collected by you! The 750-1000 A.D. silver dirhams are especially available on the market. An average circulated dirham of this period should cost about $10-$25 in average circulated condition– maybe even $10 or less, if holed or more worn. Finding a dealer who sells Islamic coins is your best bet. These Viking-Era dirhams were struck over a few centuries, but they have a consistent design type: thin-charactered Arab inscriptions on both sides, encircled by Arabic legend. Dirhams are a bit larger in diameter than a U.S. quarter, while a multiple dirham is thin and can be nearly as large in diameter as a silver dollar!

So find one of these historic silver coins, and with the cry "Vi-KINGS" ringing in your ears, admire it and know that you may be holding an example of the first– and I mean the VERY first– coin ever to cross the ocean to America!

1547-51 France Silver Douzain

CHAPTER TWENTY-SIX

A COIN OF
1564 FRENCH FLORIDA?

(1515-47 Silver Douzain Of France)

I had always assumed it was the Spanish who were the first to settle what is today the east coast of the United States. I knew St. Augustine, Florida, settled by the Spanish in 1565, was well-known for being the first permanent European settlement in the United States. What I discovered recently, however, is that there was a French fort built in present-day Florida, even before St. Augustine was founded by the Spanish! However, that French settlement, Fort Caroline, was quite short-lived. Consequently, Fort Caroline did not go down in history as the first permanent European settlement within the current United States. In that sense, Fort Caroline is somewhat like the "Lost Colony" of Roanoke Island – it was a serious attempt at colonization, but it didn't last.

Yes, there were other settlements that predated even Fort Caroline in the present-day United States. There was Spanish San Miguel de Guadalpe in 1526, and French Fort Charles, located on today's Parris Island in South Carolina, in 1562, but, as both settlements were abandoned in less than a year, they were more "footprints" than "footholds" in the New World. Then, in 1564, a group of French Protestants (also known as Huguenots) sailed to the New World to escape Catholic persecution in their home land. They settled on a spot that had been scouted out and claimed for France two years earlier. French Fort Caroline was born, and it might have survived if not for an unfortunate sequence of events.

Word soon reached King Phillip II of Spain that the French had established a settlement in the New World Florida territory, and he was none too pleased. Phillip II ordered Admiral Pedro Menendez to sail to Florida and let the French settlers know, in no uncertain terms, that Spain had laid claim to Florida, although she wasn't occupying it at the time.

Menendez and his men landed just 32 miles south of Fort Caroline, and the Spanish soon established the fort of Saint Augustine. It didn't take long for the French settlers of Fort Caroline to learn of the Spanish presence just to the south of them. Jean Ribault, the original explorer and commander of Fort Caroline, decided to take a proactive approach. He gathered all his forces and sailed south to confront the Spanish.

However, cruel fate befell the French at this point when a sudden hurricane struck. The French vessels were scattered in the storm, and finally, wrecked. Ship wreckage and victims were strewn all along the Florida coast between Fort Caroline and Saint Augustine.

Word of the French shipwrecks soon reached Menendez, who lost no time in seizing his opportunity. Knowing that Fort Caroline was now largely undefended, the Spanish made haste to seize the French fort. On September 20, 1565, Menendez captured the village, killing about 140 men and taking some 60 women and children captive. Approximately 40 to 50 French settlers somehow managed to escape by ship. With the sacking of Fort Caroline complete, the Spanish then marched down the coast, searching for survivors of the French shipwrecks. About 350 French survivors were found, captured, and hacked to death by Spanish swords.

So ended the settlement of Fort Caroline. The French would turn up again in North America in the 17th and 18th centuries, where they established a strong presence in what is today Canada and the Mississippi Valley of the United States. But there would never again be a French settlement along America's Atlantic coast.

We don't know exactly what coins, if any, came to Fort Caroline in 1564-65. In fact, we're not even certain where the fort stood — we know roughly, but not exactly. Consequently, we have no artifacts of Fort Caroline. Still, it is reasonable to assume that a coin or two or three did sail over from France to French Florida. Perhaps no coins were brought over to circulate, but I would guess some likely were brought over as souvenirs from home or to trade with the natives. So what kinds of coins would a typical settler of Fort Caroline have brought over from France?

Assuming the Huguenot settlers were of mostly humble, or possibly middle-class background, we can surmise they would have brought over the most common lower-denomi-nation coins. At the time, there were no regal copper coins struck in France. Probably the most common circulating, lower-denomination coin of mid-1560's France would be the silver douzains of Francis I (1515-47) and Henri (1547-59). These low-grade silver coins, hammered and a little larger than a U.S. quarter in diameter, featured a crowned shield with three fleur-de-lis on one side and, on the reverse, a very ornate cross with fleur-de-lis at the end of each point.

It's a little difficult getting consistent pricing on these, but at this writing, it appears that low to average circulated 1515-59 douzains should cost around $15-$30, maybe $30-$40 for a pleasant circulated example. They are not out there in huge numbers, but you can find them on eBay ("15* douzain" should be good enough for a search word) and also in the inventory of world coin dealers who sell older European hammered coins. Once you obtain one, you can proudly show it off as a coin of what could easily have been the first European settlement on the American mainland. Perhaps one day the site of Fort Caroline will be found, and excavations will reveal one or two of these 16th century douzains!

Counter-stamped 17th Century
Spanish Copper Coins

CHAPTER TWENTY-SEVEN

A COIN OF 17ᵗʰ CENTURY SPANISH GEORGIA

(1556-1665 Spanish Copper 4 Maravedis)

A few years ago, someone metal detecting on the south-eastern shore of the United States dug up an early 17ᵗʰ century Spanish copper coin, a remnant of a 16ᵗʰ century Spanish mission site. What's interesting, is that this Spanish New World artifact was not found in Florida, but in Georgia — Saint Catherine's Island, to be exact. True, "Spanish Georgia" is not news to Georgia historians, but for the rest of us it may come as a surprise to know that there was a Spanish presence in another southern Atlantic coast state BESIDES Florida! Furthermore, would it also surprise you to know that the peach, symbol of the state of Georgia, was introduced to that state, not by the British settlers who actually named the territory, "Georgia," but by the Spanish?

Spanish friars arrived in the northern part of the Florida territory, now present-day Georgia, in 1587 to establish missions and convert the local Indians to Christianity. A total of 18 missions were set up all along the coast of Georgia and on the outer islands. Then, in 1597, a Guale Indian rebellion drove the friars out of the area. For the next few years, the tiny Spanish missions sat largely abandoned. In 1605, however, the friars returned and the missions were given new life. For the next 50 years, the missions operated more or less successfully until a downswing began in the 1650's. Declining Indian populations, Indian rebellions, raids into Indian territory by Spanish soldiers and slave-raids by Indians allied with the English, all combined to hasten the abandonment of the mainland missions. By 1680, all the coastal missions of present-day Georgia were gone. Only missions located on the barrier islands were still in operation. However, in 1683 and 1684, the island missions fell prey to English pirate attacks which pretty much destroyed what was left of the Spanish missions in the region.

If you wanted a coin of "Spanish Georgia," what would be a good choice? For that, let's go back to the coin mentioned at the beginning of this chapter: the 17th century Spanish copper coin found on St. Catherine's Island off the coast of Georgia. This coin could have been a copper 4 maravedis or a 6 maravedis or an 8 maravedis — the exact denomination isn't important. Spanish copper coins of this period were often re-valued, clipped, and re-valued again due to inflation. These coins often bear multiple counter-stamps which obliterate the original design. Such pieces span the period roughly between 1556 to 1665, though the most common types seem to be from the 1621-65 period.

A few of these pieces have been discovered both in Florida and Georgia. They were probably the most commonly encountered coppers of Spanish North America during the 17th century. Silver coins, on the other hand, would have filtered up to Spanish North America from Mexico and South America, but the copper maravedis coins of 1556-1665 would have come over from Spain. As they were humble coins of the poorer classes, these coppers would certainly have been expendable enough to take to the New World wilderness by either a Spanish soldier or friar, if only as a souvenir from Spain.

Since they were struck in large numbers, a 1556-1665 Spanish 4, 6, or 8 maravedis is easily found, and many times they are even sold in small bulk! An average circulated piece will cost you anywhere from $5 to $15. Hint: on internet coin auction sites, these coins are often sold as "pirate" coins– actually a good selling point, as they were struck during the height of the Pirate Era. What's more, they have the crude look of "pirate money," or at least what many people IMAGINE "pirate money" should look like. Instead of being nicely round, these pieces are roughly hammered into squarish shapes. Some are fairly thin while others are quite thick. On the face of the coins you'll see counterstamps like, "XII" or "VIII" struck over a crouched lion or castle design. If you're lucky, you'll see a date, or at least a partial date.

Whether you seek out these coins as remnants of the Age Of Pirates, artifacts of Spanish Florida, or coins of Spanish Georgia, these crudely-struck copper coins are worth a spot in your collection!

1560-1602 British Shilling (Clipped)
of Elizabeth I

CHAPTER TWENTY-EIGHT

COINS OF
ELIZABETHAN CALIFORNIA

*(How Close Did Pebble Beach Come To Being The
First Settlement Of British North America?)*

We've already highlighted Elizabethan silver coins once, but we're going to do it again. In two cases, a 16th century Elizabethan sixpence is one of the few remnants of 1500's British California. In each case, the Elizabethan sixpence in question is controversial and poses a tantalizing historical mystery as well.

It's fairly well-documented that Sir Francis Drake and his men landed at a site just a few miles above present-day San Francisco. Some believe it was at a place known today as "Drake's Bay," though the exact landing site is still somewhat in dispute. For months, Drake and his crew explored the western coast of South America and North America on their ship, *The Golden Hind*. Their mission (in addition to looting Spanish ships and New World Spanish cities) was to find the legendary Strait of Anian, a waterway thought to connect the Pacific Ocean with the waters of the Atlantic. It's also generally accepted that Drake and his men spent about four weeks at Drake's Bay in "Nova Albion," resting, exploring, and repairing the ship.

Drake and his men finally sailed from Nova Albion, never to return. They also left no trace of their stay in northern California — or so it was thought, until 1933 when a fellow found an aged brass plate with writing on it and, fastened to a corner of the brass plate, an Elizabethan sixpence coin! The brass plate read thus:

BEE IT KNOWNE VNTO ALL MEN BY THESE PRESENTS IVNE 17, 1579 BY THE GRACE OF GOD AND IN THE NAME OF HERR MAIESTY QVEEN ELIZABETH OF ENGLAND AND HERR SVCCESSORS FOREVER I TAKE POSSESSION OF THIS KINGDOME WHOSE KING AND PEOPLE FREELY RESIGNE THEIR RIGHT AND TITLE IN THE WHOLE LAND VNTO HERR MAIESTIES KEEPEING NOW NAMED BY ME AND TO BEE KNOWN VNTO ALL MEN AS NOVA ALBION

FRANCIS DRAKE

The question remains to this day: is the brass plate authentic? Was it truly left by Sir Francis Drake in 1579? While you're pondering that, there is another much less known, Drake-in—California mystery. This one takes place in the seaside community of Pebble Beach, about a three hour drive south of Drake's Bay. Located on the Monterey Peninsula, Pebble Beach is known for its scenic shoreline, fabulous mansions and world-class golf courses. Depending on what you think about this next amazing story, Pebble Beach might ALSO have been famous as the birthplace of

British North America (a good 28 years before Jamestown took the title)!

We go back to 1934 for this story. A local resident was taking a stroll on the shores of Pebble Beach when something peculiar caught his eye: a strange, old-looking bottle half-buried in the sand. The gentleman pulled the bottle from the sand and examined it. The bottle definitely appeared to be an antique! It was also heavy, filled as it was with sand. The gentleman took the bottle home, and for the next fifteen years, it served as a bookend on his shelf!

Finally, in 1949, our Pebble Beach bottle-finder discovered that sand was now seeping out through a crack in the aged bottle. It was at this point that he decided to empty the bottle of the offending sand. In the process of emptying the bottle, he noticed two round cylinder-like objects inside the bottle. The man lost no time in enlisting the aid of a local art store owner in removing the mysterious objects. At last, with the careful use of forceps, the first object was freed from its aged container.

To the amazement of the two men, that object turned out to be a bent Elizabethan sixpence, dating back to the 1500's! Thrilled by the find, the local resident and the art store owner were even more careful removing the second object — a task that took about three hours! Finally, the second object in the bottle, a rolled-up piece of lead, was pulled out. Very deliberately, the old lead cylinder was unraveled.

There was crude writing on the lead piece. It took some time and patience to decipher, but at last the two men were able to read the etched-in message. What they read was jaw-dropping:

IN NOMINEE ELIZABETH HIBet BRITANNA
RIAR REGINA
I DO CLAIM THIS GREAT LAND AND THE SEAS
THEREOF, THERE BEING NO INHABITANTS
IN POSSESSION TO WITNESS THERETO THIS
BOTTLE AT GREAT TREE BY SMALL RIVER
AT LAT. 36 D. 30m. BEYOND HISP. FOVR OVR
MOST FAIR AND PVISSANT QVEENE AND
HERRE HEIRS AND SVCCESSORS FOREVER
VNTO THEIRR KEEPING BY GOD'S GRACE
THIS FIRST DAY OF MAY 1579

> FRANCIS DRAKE
> GENERALI
> FRANCIS FLETCHER
> Scriv

If authentic, this lead scroll was nothing less than evidence that Drake had landed at Pebble Beach and was claiming this part of North America for Great Britain — a full month before he arrived at Drake's Bay in June of 1579! Taking it a step further, if the lead scroll is to be believed, is it possible that Drake considered returning to the shores of Pebble Beach and establishing a fort? Might Drake have even contemplated establishing a colony here? Did Pebble Beach come that close to being the site of our nation's first English settlement?

Before we get too carried away, I should tell you what the experts thought of the Pebble Beach bottle, coin and lead scroll. The bottle and its contents were sent to England to be analyzed. The findings by the experts there was this: the bottle, chemically analyzed, was deemed to be at least 400 years old, placing it squarely in the Elizabethan period. Certainly, the sixpence was found to be an authentic sixpence of Elizabeth I. But the experts in England had their doubts as to the authenticity of the lead scroll and its message.

However, the lead scroll was also examined by leading university experts in California. They felt the aged lead scroll was indeed authentic. So who is to be believed? The skeptics or the believers? And where is the bottle, the coin, and the lead scroll now?

Well, the "Drake bottle" has vanished. According to the gentleman who found it, the bottle and its contents were lost when his home was burglarized in 1965. Some feel, however, that the Drake bottle, coin, and scroll are not actually lost, rather, they are being kept under wraps. Perhaps the finder was tired of the critics who insisted his prize was nothing more than an elaborate hoax. Perhaps the historical lead scroll will surface again someday. Who knows?

So.. we have Sir Francis Drake-related discoveries in central and northern California. An Elizabethan sixpence turned up in each case. Were these coins actually touched by Sir Francis Drake? Were these coins the first British coins to reach the western coast of North America? Is one of these silver coins evidence of a Drake landing on the shores of Pebble Beach? Or did some clever and enterprising person (or persons) in the 1930's track down a 400 year-old bottle, a 400 year-old coin, then engrave a historically-accurate proclamation on an old lead scroll and THEN plant the bottle in the sands of Pebble Beach? Was the authentic Elizabethan sixpence found on the brass plate at Drake's Bay also an elaborate ruse, perhaps even a ruse put over by the same person responsible for the Drake's Bay brass plate?

We have no historical documents stating that Drake landed anywhere on the Monterey Peninsula, much less at Pebble Beach. But his ship, The Golden Hind, WOULD have been in the vicinity of Pebble Beach in May of 1579, therefore, an unrecorded landing certainly would not be out of the question. Did Drake actually then sail north and leave the famous brass plate and coin at Drake's Bay the following month? We can only speculate. All I can tell you is... go find and purchase a genuine Elizabethan sixpence your-self. Remember, the cost is about $25-$40 in low to average circulated condition. Hold it in your hand, and ponder the intriguing mystery of 16th century British California!

*** A 1567 Elizabethan sixpence is also alleged to have been found near San Francisco in 1974*

1671 Sweden Copper 1/4 Ore

CHAPTER TWENTY-NINE

COINS OF SWEDISH DELAWARE

(*1633-60 Copper 1/4 Ore Of Sweden*)

Ever since 1999, a lot more people now know that Delaware became the first of our fifty United States. This knowledge came to the masses courtesy of the first State Quarter to appear in circulation: the 1999 Delaware quarter, featuring a reverse design of patriot Caesar Rodney galloping to Philadelphia to cast his vote for our nation's independence! What many folks do not realize, however, is that Delaware was first known as Nya Sverige — a colony of Sweden!

Nya Sverige, or New Sweden, was actually first settled by a Dutch contingent in 1631, but an unfortunate clash with local Indian tribes resulted in the destruction of the tiny settlement. A few years later, in 1638, Peter Minuit led a small group of Swedish settlers to Delaware Bay, where they landed and erected Fort Christina, named after Sweden's reigning child queen. This settlement was comprised of 26 men, all living in one large log house.

One of the first orders of business was to purchase 67 miles worth of land along the Delaware River from the local Lenape

Indians. Once this was done, the settlers set about planting tobacco and trading for fur pelts with the local natives. Shortly thereafter, in 1640, a ship arrived at Fort Christina bearing reinforcements and more settlers. New Sweden thrived, as some twelve expeditions arrived bearing more settlers (both Swedish and Dutch) along with more provisions. More forts were also built: Fort New Elfsborg and Fort Groteborg.

New Sweden seemed to flourish throughout the 1640's and into the 1650's. There was never a main city or even a central village since most of the settlers lived on scattered farms in small log cabins. In fact, the log cabin in America can be traced back to the colonists of New Sweden, who brought the concept over from the Old World! But though the settlers of New Sweden maintained fairly positive relations with the local Indian tribes, relations with the nearby Dutch and English settlers were decidedly strained, particularly with the Dutch.

As far back as 1641, the Dutch were angered by the New Sweden forts being built so close to their Delaware River settlements. For a time, the Dutch colonists of New Amsterdam and the Swedish colonists of New Sweden took turns conquering each other's Delaware River forts. Unfortunately, in the end, the 300 or so settlers of New Sweden were outnumbered by the Dutch.

In 1655, New Amsterdam governor, Peter Stuyvesant, acted decisively. Stuyvesant gathered a large force, including reinforcements from Old Amsterdam, and marched on New Sweden. Fort Trinity quickly fell to Stuyvesant's forces. Fort Christina held out a little longer, but finally, it too fell to the Dutch. During the latter siege, a large number of Swedish settlers had their houses and farms destroyed by the forces of Peter Stuyvesant. With the fall of Fort Christina, New Sweden's attempt at colonization came to an end. Some Swedish settlers stayed on, but they had to become subjects of New Amsterdam.

Of course, the Dutch didn't hold onto their new territory for long either. In 1664, Peter Stuyvesant was forced to surrender all of New Amsterdam to the English, and that included all the territory that was once New Sweden. It eventually became the colony of Delaware, then finally, the state of Delaware — the first state of the Union!

Happily for you, the collector, a Swedish coin from the New Sweden period should be neither terribly hard to find, nor expensive. My most logical choice for your representative coin of the New Sweden colony, is a copper 1/4 ore of Sweden, struck during the reign of Queen Christina, 1633-60. This coin, of course, very neatly corresponds to New Sweden's entire span of existence!

I have no knowledge yet of what coins, if any, have been found at New Sweden settlement sites. Still, it would seem strange if no coins came over to New Sweden on any of the twelve arriving ships. Certainly, the very agrarian settlers of New Sweden had little use for coinage, but there were probably (again) souvenir coins from the Old World. These would likely be common copper coins of the period. From the 1600's through the 1700's, Sweden was a leading producer of copper in Europe, so we have many Swedish copper coins of this era from which to choose.

Prices: a 1633-60 1/4 ore of Sweden should only cost $7-$15 in average circulated condition, $15-$20 in pleasant circulated condition. And I'm actually adding on a few dollars from recent catalogue values, which shows how affordable these old coins are! The smaller copper 1/6 ore of 1666-86 (remember, the Swedish presence in Delaware lingered on after 1655) is just as cheap. The larger ½ copper ore of 1628-31 is also affordable at $10-$20 in average circulated condition, $20-$25 in pleasant circulated condition. Again, search for them on eBay and other internet auction sites, as well as from dealers of older world coins.

1789 France Copper Sol of Louis XVI

CHAPTER THIRTY

COIN OF A PENNSYLVANIA FRENCH ROYALIST SETTLEMENT

(1778-91 Copper Sol Of France)

About ten miles south of Towanda, Pennsylvania, there is an open meadow that slopes down from the forested hills of western Pennsylvania. A bend of the Susquehanna River half encircles this peaceful meadow. A couple of 19th century houses can be seen nearby. The ruins of an old mill house are also visible at this scenic, pastoral spot. Aside from the surrounding natural beauty, there is nothing about this place that seems particularly remarkable. Unless, of course, you happen to know the history of this now-tranquil meadow. Then you would know that this rural sloped terrace was once the site of a French royalist settlement, and COULD have been (had history gone a little differently) the home of deposed French Queen Marie Antoinette and her two children. The settlement of French New Azilum (or Asylum) was first settled in the fall of 1793 by French refugees. These refugees, many of them loyalists to the French monarchy, fled France to escape imprisonment and death at the hands of French revolutionaries. Also among the French refugees were those fleeing a violent slave uprising in Santo Domingo. Fortunately, the French exiles had sympathizers in the Philadelphia area. In particular, three men of influence, Stephen Girard, Robert Morris, and John Nicholson, purchased a large tract of land in the northern part of Pennsylvania; 1600 acres in all were laid aside for the new settlement. New Azilum was born.

Construction of a town began at once. Some 300 acres were set aside for the town plot, complete with a two-acre market square and streets laid out in a gridiron pattern. By the spring of 1794, 30 log houses were built. In short order, several small shops, a schoolhouse, and theater appeared. Dairy farming and sheep-raising were important settlement enterprises. Orchards and gardens were also planted. New Azilum had its own gristmill, blacksmith shop and distillery. Although the housing structures were somewhat crude, features were added for beautification, such as chimneys, wallpaper, window glass, and window shutters.

The most dominant of the New Azilum structures was "La Grande Maison," a two-story log structure that was 84 feet long and 60 feet wide. La Grande Maison had numerous small-paned windows and eight fireplaces. It served as a hotel for important guests. It was also a place where social gatherings were held. Among the VIP guests at La Grande Maison was Louis Phillipe, later to become King of France!

La Grande Maison is fascinating for another reason. The grand house was said to have been built for the Queen of France herself, Marie Antoinette, and her two children. The fact that this structure was built on such an imposing scale seems to lend credence to the story. Unfortunately, Marie Antoinette did not escape the French Revolution. She was beheaded in 1793. Had she been able to flee France, she might well have found refuge in New Azilum!

Despite the safety and tranquility for the French exiles in the Pennsylvania countryside, economic hardship struck. Two New Azilum financial backers, Robert Morris and John Nicholson, went bankrupt. Income from French sources dried up. By the late 1790's, many of the New Azilum immigrants were on the move to American cities in the south, such as Charleston, Savannah, and New Orleans. Others returned to Santo Domingo on the island of Haiti, after things quieted down there. Even more New Azilum settlers were lost when Napoleon made it possible for French Revolution exiles to return to France. By 1803, New Azilum was no more. Today, not one of the fifty settlement structures remain.

Just what kind of coin or coins might a resident of New Azilum have brought with them to the hill country of Pennsylvania? Silver and copper coins of Louis XVI would be my first guess. Certainly the settlers of New Azilum were loyal to the crown, so they would have no problem carrying the king's coin! My vote for most likely coin carried over from France to New Azilum would be the very common copper 1 sol of Louis XVI, struck 1778-91. Certainly a few early 1770's copper sols and half-sols from late in Louis XV's reign might have come over as well. A copper 1 sol of 1778-91 will set you back around $5-$10 in average circulated condition. The smaller half-sol and larger two-sol of Louis XVI are also easy to find. The brass two-sol is a fairly large, thick coin and will cost around $10-$20 in average circulated condition.

Just as an added bit of trivia —and this has nothing to do with New Azilum —any coin of Louis XVI COULD have been the very coin that cost the king his head! In the midst of the French Revolution, Louis XVI decided it would be prudent to flee Paris. He boarded a coach with his family. Unfortunately, en route to the village of Varennes, where

Louis was to join troops loyal to the crown, a man recognized the king and turned him in! It seems the man had recognized Louis' profile from seeing it on the face of a coin! Poor Louis was taken into custody, returned to Paris, and subsequently, lost his head to the guillotine.

CHAPTER THIRTY-ONE

COINS FROM A COLONIAL MASSACHUSETTS "GHOST TOWN"

W e've already discussed a coin that was surely seen in the shops and trading posts of 1692 Salem, Massachusetts. In this chapter, we visit another Colonial Massachusetts locale, one that has its own tales of witch lore. Unlike the town of Salem, which still thrives to this day, this village was deserted long ago. The coins left behind at the site of this Colonial ghost town, however, have just started to come out of the ground, thanks to the use of modern metal detectors. During the writing of this book, I was fortunate enough to purchase a small lot of these until-recently buried coins — fifteen coppers to be exact. It took a good deal of metal brushing, olive oil cleaning, and squinting under bright lights before I could ascertain the true identities of the corroded, muck-covered coppers I'd purchased, but what I found was quite fascinating.

THE SITE:

"Dogtown" has been deserted since the early 1830's. Local historians believe it was first settled in 1719, though other accounts indicate there was a small community at the site as early as 1650. The site of Dogtown is located just inland from the coastal port town of Gloucester, Massachusetts. Indeed, Dogtown was not so much a town unto itself as it was an inland "'burb" of Gloucester. The town of Gloucester was founded in 1623, just three years after the Pilgrims landed at Plymouth. That makes Gloucester not only one of the oldest settlements in Massachusetts, but in the entire United States as well!

From her earliest days, Gloucester was a major shipping and fishing port. In fact, British ships would sail hundreds of miles just to fish the incredibly bountiful Atlantic waters of Cape Ann. Consequently, the earliest settlers of Gloucester were sailors, fishermen and their families. But in the mid-1600's or early 1700's, depending on which account you believe — an inland community began developing away from the seaside settlement of Gloucester. It wasn't called Dogtown at the time, that would come later. The point is, this community was built amongst the trees, low hills and rock-laden terrain that lay just to the west of Gloucester. And rather than being settled by sailors and fishermen, Dogtown was said to be a community of farmers and land-workers.

It is estimated that the inland settlement reached its peak in the years just before the Revolutionary War. Then, the village began to lose a good portion of the male population, as men marched away to fight the British. The women were left behind. To protect themselves and their homes, many of village's wives and mothers made sure they secured the services of a good guard dog. In addition to the wives of farmers and soldiers, however, it is said there were also widows and never-married women who lived alone in this inland community. A few of these women were whispered to be practicing witchcraft amidst the trees and boulders of Gloucester's inland community. Were these stories true? We'll probably never know for sure; it was not uncommon for odd or eccentric single women in Colonial times to gain unearned reputations as "witches."

Starting in the 1780's or so, the population of Dogtown began to dwindle. It is believed the village was completely abandoned by 1832. Abandoned, that is, save for the population of dogs that scampered in and about the empty houses and buildings. Hence, the settlement is known to this day as Dogtown.

If you visit the Dogtown site today, you will find mostly trees, some trails and a perplexing maze of rocks and boulders. In fact, it is not recommended that hikers and joggers venture into the Dogtown" area alone, especially not those unfamiliar with the area, for it is quite easy to get lost. All that's left of the old village itself are a few foundations and cellar holes. As it was in Colonial times, Dogtown remains a most mysterious place.

THE COINS FOUND:

Without further ado, these are the coins of my fifteen-piece Dogtown, Massachusetts lot:

Four 1694 British Halfpennies of William & Mary: This was truly surprising. Four out of fifteen copper coins were identified as William & Mary halfpennies, the most of any one coin type in this grouping. It's unusual for as I stated before, the earliest British coppers to come to America in quantity were the 1695-1701 British halfpennies. Do these 4 William & Mary halfpence disprove that theory? I still don't think so: these four relatively scarce halfpenny types could easily have come over as many as 50 years after they were struck, as opposed to coming over to Massachusetts during the years they were current (and in this case, that would ONLY be in 1694).

1695-1701 British Halfpenny of William III: Not surprising to see a William III halfpenny in this lot, for as we learned earlier, a pretty decent supply of these did indeed circulate in Colonial America.

1740-59 British Halfpenny of George II: The only surprise here is that *more* of my fifteen coppers weren't George II halfpence.

1787-88 Mystery Copper: Possibly a Massachusetts Cent of 1787-88 or perhaps even the much rarer Immunis Columbia pattern copper. Only a partial eagle wing can be seen on this much-corroded copper coin..

1785-6 Vermont 'Landscape' Copper: A very popular and pretty scarce copper coin struck when Vermont was actually still its own republic! I was pleasantly surprised to see the design of this coin emerge when I cleaned it, worn though it is.

1787 Fugio Cent: Wow! A classic coin that (if you recall from very early in the book) is actually the first coin authorized by the Unites States of America. Quite corroded, but here too, a definite keeper.

1740-87 Mystery Copper/New Jersey Cent(?): A very corroded piece that, upon heavy metal brushing, appears to have a shield on one side that very much resembles the shield on the reverse of the 1786-87 New Jersey state coppers. I could be wrong—it could still be a British Halfpence or counterfeit halfpence of George II or III.

1820's Coronet Head Large Cent: Dogtown was deserted around 1832, so this U.S. large cent type would have been in circulation at the time. Horribly corroded.

c. 1870's Canada Prince Edward Island Halfpenny: Hmmm, this coin was struck somewhat after the time Dogtown was said to have been completely abandoned. But then, that doesn't mean human history stopped at the site. Hikers, hunters, campers have no doubt filtered through the vicinity all through the years, hence, the explanation for this coin.

Mystery Copper or Brass Coin: Too big and thin in diameter to be any kind of British coin or, in my opinion, even a counterfeit. Appears to be a hammered piece, thus would date early to mid 1600's possibly. Chipped, corroded and worn virtually to nothing, this green mystery piece is the most intriguing of the lot. My wild theory: size and module-wise, it seems to me it *could* be a rare 1616 Bermuda 'Hog Money' Shilling, the first coins struck for the British New World (depicting a hog on one side, a ship on the other). Wishful thinking perhaps?

The final two copper pieces are too worn to identify. Either could be a British halfpenny of George II-III, a counterfeit thereof, or a 1785-88 state copper.

CONCLUSIONS:

The make-up of this fifteen-coin group was truly eye opening. As I mentioned before, I would not have expected *four* William & Mary halfpennies to be found at a small Colonial Massachusetts site! It would be interesting to know at what point they came over from England to America! But beyond that, I was astonished at the VARIETY of copper coins found in this fifteen-coin lot: four William & Mary halfpence, a William III halfpence, a George II halfpence, at LEAST four different state/confederation coppers of the 1780's (maybe as many as 7 if I could identify the others), an 1820's U.S. large cent and a Canadian coin from the 1870's. That's an amazing variety of coins coming from one little inland village in northern Massachusetts! And I don't think the seller was mixing in a variety for my customer satisfaction: virtually all of these coins were unidentifiable before cleaning. What I was expecting to see: mostly George II-III British halfpennies of 1740-75, maybe a William III halfpence or two, and if I was lucky, a Connecticut and/or Massachusetts copper of the 1780's.

So what can we conclude from this fifteen-coin Dogtown, Massachusetts lot? A lot would depend on whether these coins were found in one spot, or scattered throughout the vicinity. Unfortunately, I don't have specific information as to just where in the vicinity of Dogtown these coins were found. If they were indeed found in one spot, I would conclude that these coins belonged to one owner, a late 18th century or early 19th century Dogtown resident who probably enjoyed accumulating low denomination coins of varying types (though the inclusion of the 1870's Canadian coin doesn't fit neatly into this theory).

In the more likely event these coppers were found scattered throughout the Dogtown site and outlying areas, perhaps we can conclude that a wide variety of coins, or at least copper coins, circulated in Dogtown during its dying years. And it would follow that so many of the coins found would be coppers — after all, these were the coin of the common man. The residents of Dogtown were not the wealthy, nor the high-status individuals of the Cape Ann region of Massachusetts, especially from the late 1700's to early 1800's.

I also can't help but wonder if the five oldest coins (at least the identifiable ones), the William & Mary and William III coppers, actually circulated in Dogtown in the late 1600's, or if they came to the settlement years after. I am inclined to think the latter scenario is true, but I wouldn't swear to it. If these coppers did circulate in the late 1600's, then these are genuine relics that witnessed Colonial Massachusetts history in the years just following the Salem witch hysteria of 1692!

BONUS:
A FEW UNDER-RATED 'RED BOOK' RECOMMENDATIONS

Up until now I've been discussing lost, forgotten, and overlooked coin treasures of early America. As a general rule, I've spurned the "*Red Book*" coins as overlooked treasures. My reasoning was simple enough. If they're listed in A Guide Book of United States Coins, they're not secrets. BUT, that doesn't mean there aren't overlooked coins that are listed in the *Red Book*, coins that deserve more acclaim and collector demand than they do. Such coins are often referred to as "sleepers," coins that, once the collecting public wises up to their true worth, will awaken and SOAR in value! Of course, some sleepers never really wake up, but that's another story.

Since this book is about the coins of early America, the following bonus chapters will highlight coins from the Colonial, Federation, and early U.S. periods. The earliest of these coins was struck nearly 10 years before the birth of George Washington. The most recent circulated in the last years of Thomas Jefferson's life. At this moment, the value of each coin featured is certainly rising in value at a greater pace than the coins featured in previous chapters. Yet, in my opinion, each one still represents a great value for the money. They're still available. They're still affordable, even with prices going up slowly, but steadily. So... let's get on with the show.

1723 Wood's Hibernia Farthing

CHAPTER THIRTY-TWO

1722-24 WOOD'S HIBERNIA HALFPENNIES & FARTHINGS

O pen up <u>A Guide Book of United States Coins</u> (other-wise known as the *Red Book*) and look over the section featuring the coins of Colonial and Early America. There are a lot of them listed. A LOT! But look closer. Only a small portion of the coins listed were actually struck in the Colonial period! You'll find a myriad of state coins and privately-struck tokens that were struck in the 1780's and 1790's. Some of the coins and tokens featured date AFTER the U.S. Mint was established and cranking out coins! What does this mean? It means your options for obtaining a *Red-Book*-listed Colonial coin– a TRUE Colonial-era coin, are rather limited.

Now take a closer look at these *Red Book* Colonials, the ones dated between 1652 and 1776.Look at the prices for a good many of them! Want a 1600's New England silver coin? Want a 1694 Elephant token? Want a 1737 Connecticut Higley token? Want a 1776 Continental dollar? For these and other true Colonial coins listed in the *Red Book*, we're talking at least a few hundred dollars; in other cases, thousands! But don't despair– there are a few very nicely affordable *Red Book* Colonials. And the Wood's Hibernia coppers are as affordable as they come.

What in the world is a Wood's Hibernia coin? Here's the story. In 1722, William Wood secured a royal contract that would allow him to strike copper halfpenny and farthing tokens for Ireland. This was a similar situation to that in the early 1600's, when private parties secured royal patents to strike farthings and circulate them as coins of the realm (remember the Harrington farthings of the James I period?). So, for three years, 1722-24, William Wood struck copper halfpennies and farthings with the following design: a wigged bust of George I on the obverse, and on the reverse, a seated Britannia figure with harp (the symbol of Ireland). At the same time, Wood secured ANOTHER royal contract to strike brass two pence tokens to be used in the American Colonies! These pieces came to be known as the Rosa Americana tokens, and they are also featured in the *Red Book*. But that's another story.

Almost immediately, William Wood's copper tokens were rejected in Ireland. The citizens of Ireland were insulted by this pathetic gesture by the British crown to provide them with copper coinage. Why? Because the halfpenny and farthing tokens were underweight, clearly substandard compared to the heavier, sturdier British halfpenny and farthing coins of George I. The William Wood coinage was so thoroughly rejected in Ireland that British authorities decided they had to come up with some other use for the prodigious output of Wood's Hibernia coppers. They didn't have to think for long.

From the earliest years of British settlement in America, the colonists had hungered for small-change coin denominations. They made numerous requests for small-denomination coinage. "So," reasoned the British authorities, "why not send the Hibernia copper tokens to America?" And so it was done– apparently. I say apparently because there is no real document that indicates a large shipment of Wood's Hibernia coppers was sent to America. Some numismatists dispute that any such large shipment of Wood's Hibernia coppers came over. Still, these tokens have turned up in Colonial coin accumulations; hence, the Wood's Hibernia coppers are considered a valid "Colonial" coin of America.

Having been struck in the years 1722-24, the Wood's Hibernia tokens' period of circulation falls well within the Colonial period. In fact, they were struck a good ten years before George Washington was born! Furthermore, despite Ireland's complaints about their being underweight, the Wood's Hibernia coppers were actually well-made pieces and many of them have survived in pretty good shape. I've always preferred the Wood's Hibernia token bust portrait of George I to the George I bust on the British halfpence and farthings of the same period. So what you have, in my opinion, is a winning combination: a true Colonial-era coin with a fairly attractive design. You could say that Ireland's loss is your collection's gain!

You'd think a Colonial coin struck in the 1720's would come with a hefty price tag. But the Wood's Hibernia coppers, both the farthing and the halfpenny, are the cheapest of ALL the coins and tokens listed in the Colonial/Early America section of the *Red Book*! The obvious reason for this is that these tokens have survived in fairly large numbers. They are not hard to track down. Still, that doesn't tell the whole story. If there was more demand, these tokens would NOT be so available, hence the prices would be much higher. But there is not a lot of demand for these coppers. Why would that be?

My theory is that U.S. collectors generally consider these tokens to be "Irish" pieces. Collectors of U.S. Colonial coins are much more prone to gravitate towards coins with which they can identify, such as Massachusetts silver coins, American Plantation tokens, and the state coppers of the 1780's. As a result, prices for Wood's Hibernia tokens remain affordable: $15-$35 in low to decent circulated condition! Folks, that's cheaper than a good many U.S. coins minted in the 1900's (and 20th century coins were struck in much larger numbers)! That's why I feel these Wood's Hibernia classics of the 1720's are highly under-rated and deserving of mention!

1773 Virginia Halfpenny

CHAPTER THIRTY-THREE

AN AFFORDABLE, ONE OF A KIND COLONIAL COIN!

(*1773 Virginia Halfpenny*)

Of all the Colonial and Confederation-Era coins listed in the *Red Book*, I believe the 1773 Virginia halfpenny is the most under-rated. Any collector or dealer who has done a general overview of American Colonial coins is familiar with the 1773 Virginia halfpenny. The problem is, I think most collectors and even dealers, miss the real significance of this coin. Most collectors view the 1773 Virginia half-penny as simply one of the state copper coins of the late 18th century, albeit an earlier one than the Vermont, New Jersey, Connecticut, New York and Massachusetts issues.

But the Virginia halfpenny stands out for more than just its Colonial-era 1773 date. This coin is the ONLY official Colonial coin struck by the royal crown specifically for use in the American Colonies! This coin stands alone amongst the many, many coin and token types listed under the heading of "Colonial Coins."

Great Britain had FINALLY heeded the call of the Colonies for regal hard money, and authorized a coinage for the colony of Virginia. Featuring a bust of George III on the obverse and a crowned shield of arms on the reverse, these copper halfpence were struck, presumably, at the London Tower Mint in 1773, then shipped to Virginia. There was some delay, however, in the shipment of these coins. They didn't arrive until 1774. They were not distributed, however, until 1775. Not the best timing. It was a period of upheaval in the Colonies. Tensions with Britain had peaked – after all, it was the very eve of the American Revolution. British troops and American colonists had already exchanged gunfire at Bunker Hill in Massachusetts. In a year's time, the Colonies would declare their independence. Some Virginia halfpennies circulated briefly, but soon were hoarded by nervous colonists.

For the remainder of the 1770's and into the first years of the 1780's, the Revolutionary War raged. At last, British General, Lord Cornwallis surrendered to General George Washington at Yorktown in Virginia. For all practical purposes, the war was over. America had achieved independence from Britain!

Independent or not, America was still a coin-poor country. George III may not have been recognized as king any longer, but that didn't keep Americans from accepting coins with his profile on them! In fact, when the states had the authority to strike their own copper coins in 1785, they mostly struck coins copying the designs of George II and George III coppers! Into this coin-hungry climate, the Virginia halfpennies returned to circulation around 1781, shortly after the surrender of the British at Yorktown. This was no small irony, considering these coins were the only coins truly meant to be "Colonial" issues!

The Virginia halfpennies survive today in either low to average condition, or near mint-state condition. This is because the ones that did reach circulation, circulated a LOT, as was typical of workhorse copper coins. However, at least one keg worth of Virginia halfpence did NOT circulate. In the mid-1800's, a keg full of uncirculated Virginia halfpennies was discovered– about 2,200 pieces! The coins from this hoard were sold off to collectors over the years. As a result, a significant number of Virginia coppers survive in mint-state or near mint-state today.

Prices are still amazingly low considering the one-of-a-kind status of this Colonial coin. A low circulated piece can probably be secured for $20-$35, an average circulated example for $35-$50. It's actually one of the LEAST expensive of the 18th century Colonial and early United States coins! Add this coin to your collection now! Besides, how can you resist a coin that passed from hand to hand on the Virginia streets of Alexandria, Richmond, Williamsburg and Yorktown?

1785 Nova Constellation Token

CHAPTER THIRTY-FOUR

A COULD-HAVE-BEEN FIRST UNITED STATES COIN!

(1783-85 Nova Constellatio Tokens)

"I'd just like to say thank you on behalf of the group and myself, and I hope we passed the audition."

John Lennon spoke these words after the last song on the last album released by the Beatles. Ironic words. Passed the audition? The Beatles were about to go out as the greatest group in pop music history. Of COURSE they passed the audition!

Well, the Beatles may not have had to pass an audition (at least not that late in their careers), but coin designs do! We see that today when numerous artists submit their ideas for the new state quarters. The selection committee then has to decide the following: is the design too cluttered? Is the design too sparse? Does the design have a certain beauty and eye appeal to it? Does the design accurately encapsulate the ideals and/or history of the United States (or in the case of the state quarters, the state itself)? Will people find the design offensive? Does the design leave enough room for the required legends, date and inscriptions? Is the design even coin-able? These are just a few of the considerations that must be weighed before the United States Mint gives the OK to create a newly designed coin.

This was true in the earliest days of the fledgling United States, even before an official United States Mint existed. Following the Treaty of Versailles in 1783, which officially liberated the United States from the yoke of Great Britain, one of the first tasks at hand was to create a coinage suitable for what we were in 1783: a confederation of states. So the question was this: would our nation have a coinage that would circulate across states, or would each state strike their own coins? As it turned out, the state coinage idea won out, hence, from 1785 through 1788, Connecticut, Massachusetts, New York and New Jersey were striking their own copper coins while the other, less decisive states, continued to make do with the hodge-podge of foreign coins they'd been using for years.

Still, it was no secret that the newly established Congress of the United States had an eye towards a truly national coinage. Consequently, a few ambitious souls came forward to "audition" their designs and concepts for a national coinage. One such audition was the introduction of the Nova Constellatio patterns.

There are actually two distinct Nova Constellatio issues: the first, the silver decimal issues, are what most numismatists regard as the OFFICIAL Nova Constellatio pattern coins. These Nova Constellatio pattern coins were struck in silver and had decimal values visible on them, decimals based on a system of 1,000 (as opposed to our current dollar system based on a decimal system of 100). These silver patterns were proposed by Gouverneur Morris of New York, who also proposed that the United States coinage use his decimal system based on 1,000. The design featured an eye centered within a bursting star on one side, the initials "U.S." within a wreath and the decimal value on the other. But our discussion of the silver Nova Constellation patterns is strictly academic — you won't find them, you can't afford them. They are too rare and too costly. BUT... the *other* Nova Constellatio pieces, the ones struck in copper, are indeed available and affordable!

First a note of caution: many experts don't consider the Nova Constellatio coppers of 1783-85 to be a pattern coinage. The silver Nova Constellatios, yes, the coppers, no. Said experts would tell you that the Nova Constellatio coppers are tokens with designs based ON the official silver Nova Constellatio patterns. What's more, the Nova Constellatio coppers were not struck in America, but rather in Birmingham, England, once again, at the behest and expense of Gouverneur Morris! They were then exported to America, and, due to their American-theme design, saw circulation here as a token coinage.

What did the Nova Constellatio coppers look like? Just like the 1783 silver pattern Nova Constellatios, but minus the decimal value on them. The reverse design of the 1785 Nova Constellatio coppers was modified somewhat, when the block letter "U.S." within the wreath became a very cursive "U.S." within the wreath. Which brings up an interesting point about these pieces: they were the first circulating coins (of a type) to allude to the newly formed 'United States' on the face of the coin — if only in initial form! That's a pretty major first!

And getting back to our audition theme: true, we may have to draw a distinct line between the official silver pattern Nova Constellatio coins and these similarly designed copper tokens that came just after. Although we can't give the copper Nova Constellatio pieces full-fledged U.S. coin pattern status, they can still consider these circulating copper tokens to be a definite audition. As a fairly successful circulating "coin," the attractive Nova Constellatio design got great publicity and "face time" before the American public. No doubt, Gouverneur Morris hoped favorable word of mouth might prompt the United States Congress to adopt his Nova Constellatio design for our nation's first coinage!

Alas, it was not to be. The state coppers continued to be the only American-produced coins from 1785 through 1787, until finally, in 1787, the United States Congress authorized 300 tons of "Fugio cents" to be struck by a private contractor — although not anywhere close to 300 tons of Fugio cents were actually produced, but that's another story. The point is, the 1787 Fugio cent became the first officially authorized coin of the Unites States of America, not the Nova Constellatio coins. Still, the Nova Constellation coppers remain to this day, an obtainable and affordable example of a "First Might-Have Been U.S. Coin." There were other pre-1787 U.S. coin patterns, but probably none, in my opinion, stood as much chance of being adopted as the Nova Constellatio pieces.

So why are the Nova Constellatio coppers of 1783-85 still under-rated? Another of my theories: collectors flipping through the *Red Book* are presented with a perplexing array of coins and tokens from the 1780's. The Nova Constellatio coppers are noticed by U.S. Colonial coin collectors to be sure, but I don't think many of these collectors realize the Novas represent an important pattern – or "audition," if you prefer — for our first national coinage. I think many collectors still see the Nova Constellatio coppers as simply one of a number of tokens with American-theme designs, that were struck in England, and sent over here to circulate — just like, say, the 1781 North American tokens or the George Washington tokens.

Because collectors of Colonial and early U.S. coins generally know about the Nova Constellatio coppers, these pieces don't exactly fly under the radar unnoticed. Prices have been going up steadily for these coins since the advent of the internet, state quarters, and eBay, as is the case with pretty much all *Red Book*-featured Colonial and early U.S. coins. Right now, around $40-$60 should get you a low circulated Nova Constellatio token of 1783 or 1785. That price range may not stand for even another year, even for low grade pieces. That means the time to jump on these coppers is NOW! That price range is a bit more than other coins featured in this book, but I feel that's a bargain price considering what you get for your money.

Consider: this is a token whose design received legitimate consideration to be the "face" of the first United States coinage. This is the first circulating coinage (of sorts) to prominently display the proud initials, "U.S." on the face of the coin. In addition, the Nova Constellatio pieces bear the proud slogans, "Libertas" and "Justititia" (that's Latin for Liberty and Justice in case you were wondering) just so American citizens of the 1780's would not be in the dark as to what principals their new country stood for! So whether you consider the Nova Constellatio tokens an important pattern coin or simply a possible audition piece, I think these tokens are still too attractively priced today to pass up.

1816 U.S. Coronet Head Large Cent

CHAPTER THIRTY-FIVE

AFFORDABLE THOMAS JEFFERSON-ERA COINS

(1816-20 Coronet Head Large Cents)

A s mentioned in an earlier chapter, when we think of
famous American "Founding Fathers," three names
leap immediately to most people's minds: George Washington,
Benjamin Franklin, and, of course, Thomas Jefferson.
Jefferson is still a well-known figure. His face appears on
the U.S. nickel. And most Americans (hopefully) know that
Jefferson was not only one of our first Presidents, but he
also penned the Declaration of Independence. Anyone with
a rudimentary knowledge of American history also knows
that Jefferson is responsible for the 1803 Louisiana Purchase
which extended our nation's territory south and west.

Even though we associate Jefferson with the Colonial
era, he lived well past the period when our country was
made up of only thirteen British Colonies. Thomas Jefferson
died in 1826, at the ripe old age of 83. To the very end, this
Renaissance Man pursued his love of science, nature, philos-

ophy, and architecture. Not only did Jefferson design the still-stunning architectural marvel of a home, Monticello, but he is also responsible for designing many of the buildings at the University of Virginia. Founding Father, President of the United States, and overall genius– the remarkable Thomas Jefferson was all of these.

Acquiring a U.S. coin struck during the lifetime of Thomas Jefferson is quite do-able for the budget-minded collector. Affordable –maybe not cheap, but affordable – Jefferson-Era U.S. coins are available in the Draped Bust and Classic Head half cent series, the Draped Bust large cent series, the Capped Bust dime series, and the Capped Bust Quarter series. However, your most affordable Jefferson-Era U.S. coin will likely be a Coronet Head large cent.

The Coronet Head large cents were struck from 1816 to 1839. Only a couple of dates in the series are particularly scarce, those being the 1821 and 1823 cents. That means all the Coronet Head cents struck during the last years of Jefferson's life, 1816-26, are well within the means of the cost-conscious collector. In fact, the 2006 retail values for any Coronet Head large cent dated 1816-26, are pretty consistent across the board. For any of these dates, you can expect to pay $20-$35 for a piece in low to average circulated condition– maybe $30-$45 for the 1816 date. Even in the lower grades, these large cents should have readable dates.

The Coronet Head large cent is not actually considered an early U.S. coin type. U.S. collectors, particularly those that collect early U.S. copper, consider 1815 to be the cut-off date for the "Early U.S." designation. But the earliest years of the Coronet Head cent do span what many other collectors consider to be the Early U.S. period, and that would be any U.S. coin struck up to and including 1820. Personally, I like 1820 as the cutting-off-date for Early U.S.. For one thing, 1820 is a nice even number. Secondly, no less than three key Revolutionary War figures were still alive in 1820: Thomas

Jefferson, John Adams, and King George III (the monarch to whom Jefferson addressed the Declaration Of Independence in 1776)! Thirdly, 1820 is just one scant generation removed from the lifetime of George Washington, who died in 1799.

Actually, the dates of 1816 and 1817 could be particularly worthwhile when it comes to seeking a Jefferson-Era Coronet Head large cent. And it's not just because those are the two earliest dates of the series! If you have a *Red Book* handy, or any other value guide of U.S. coins, you will notice something interesting. There are not U.S. silver coins of any denomination with the date of 1816! In fact, there are no *gold* coins with a date of 1816! As for the 1817-dated coins, there is only one U.S. silver coin with that date: the 1817 Capped Bust half dollar. No U.S. gold coins are dated 1817. Yet, in those two years, the U.S. Mint struck just under 3 million large cents dated 1816, and just under 4 million 1817 large cents! So why did the U.S. Mint strike so many large cents in 1816 and 1817, while completely ignoring half dimes, dimes, quarters, dollars, and all gold coins?

Someone who has studied the history of Spanish-Colonial silver coins circulating in the early United States could offer this explanation: in the years spanning 1806-20, the U.S. Mint virtually ceased making all silver coin denominations (save for the half dollar in 1817) because of a huge influx of Spanish silver coins into this country! The U.S. Mint could not compete with the popular, fine-silver Spanish coins struck at the mints of Mexico City and Lima, Peru (among others). The large number of Spanish ½,1, 2, and 8 reales meant there was no demand for U.S. half dimes, dimes, quarters and dollars. That would seem to explain the lack of U.S. silver coins dated 1816 and 1817. But that's not actually the true story behind the cent-dominated years of 1816 and 1817.

Fire! The bane of our ancestors (though not as deadly as rampant disease and sickness, to be sure). In the old days, buildings generally didn't meet their end by virtue of demolition– it was usually by fire. History is FILLED with fire: houses burning, public buildings burning, entire cities burning! Sometimes an invading army was to blame. More often, however, it was the accident-waiting-to-happen mixture of wooden structures, candles, fireplaces, and wood-burning stoves (and no smoke alarms to speak of). In any event, an outbuilding of the early U.S. Mint in Philadelphia caught fire in January of 1816. All the rolling mills used to roll out planchets for silver and gold coins were destroyed or damaged beyond use. New machinery would have to be procured and installed, but that would take some time. What to do in the meantime? You can't make silver or gold coins, but you CAN make copper coins! So they minted large cents.

And now you know the rest of the story. Some 3 million 1816 large cents (a large mintage for that period) came pouring out of the Philadelphia mint, followed by some 4 million 1817-dated large cents. Were it not for the fire of January 1816, the 1816 and 1817 Coronet Head large cents would likely have been struck in smaller numbers, and thus, been more scarce than they are today.

1820 U.S. Capped Bust Dime

CHAPTER THIRTY-SIX

AFFORDABLE
EARLY U.S. SILVER COINS

(1814 & 1820 Capped Bust Dimes)

Early U.S. silver coins. They're historical. They're scarce. They're sought-after. They're for the advanced or "serious" collector. They're expensive! All true – in a general sense. Also, generally speaking, "early U.S. silver" would be the Flowing Hair or Draped Bust type half dimes, dimes, quarters, half dollars and dollars. In other words, they would be U.S. silver coins struck between 1794 and 1807. All these coins are indeed expensive, "expensive" being a relative term, as always. Your best bet for 1794-1807 U.S. silver would be either an 1803-07 Draped Bust half dollar or an 1805-07 Draped Bust quarter, both of which cost $200-$250 in average circulated condition as of this writing.

There is, however, a viable early U.S. silver alternative. As I've mentioned in the previous chapter, many collectors are upping the "Early U.S." period to 1820, or even up into 1830! If you're willing to at least include the years 1807-20 in your Early U.S. time frame, then you have a few more affordable and obtainable options for your early U.S. coin collection. Again, using the Thomas Jefferson, John Adams, King George III triad as your barometer, you might consider 1820 and before as "early" U.S. So what kinds of silver coins was the United States Mint churning out around 1820? Capped Bust silver coins – half dimes, dimes, quarters, and half dollars (no silver dollars were struck during this period). Capped Bust silver coins are certainly more affordable and obtainable than the earlier Draped Bust and Flowing Hair silver coin types. I've chosen two Capped Bust silver coins in particular to discuss: the 1814 and 1820 Capped Bust dimes. At this point you may be asking, "What about the dimes struck 1815 to 1819?" There were no dimes struck during those years. Remember, a combination of factors resulted in the scarce and sporadic minting of U.S. dimes in the early 1800's: an influx of Spanish silver coins into this country, as well as the nasty U.S. Mint fire that occurred in the first month of 1816!

Of the two dates we'll be discussing, I think the 1814 Bust dime is a good deal more desirable. And it's not JUST because the 1814 dime is obviously older than the 1820 dime. More to the point, the 1814 Bust dime is scarcer– mintage for the 1814 dime is 421,500 while 942,587 dimes were struck with an 1820 date. In my opinion, however, it's not just a matter of age and scarcity. Two key factors truly weigh heavier in favor of the 1814 Bust dime: history and its favorable scarcity/value ratio.

First, we'll take a look at the history aspect. With the 1814 Bust dime you get a coin struck in the early part of the 1810's, thus making the 1814 dime an even stronger candidate for "early" U.S. coin status. In fact, there is a good-sized segment of the numismatic community that views the year 1815– not 1820, not 1830– as the cut-off year for the title of "early" U.S. coin. That view is mainly based on the large cents: the last "early" large cent, the Classic Head type, was struck in 1814, while the first non-early or "classic" large cent, the Coronet Head type, was struck in 1816. Personally, I still prefer my "Jefferson-Adams-George III" barometer, but then.. oh, well. In any event, the 1814 Capped Bust dime does indeed make the cut according to a very widely-held numismatic definition of "Early U.S. Coin."

I like the 1814 Capped Bust Dime for another reason— it's a War Of 1812 coin! Yes, the War Of 1812 actually lasted until 1815, the year American troops, fighting under General Andrew Jackson, defeated the British at the Battle Of New Orleans. It was a great victory for the Americans, but unnecessary. "Old Hickory," Andrew Jackson, had not yet received the news that the Treaty Of Ghent had already been signed! But 1814 was a pivotal year in that conflict. In the year of 1814 the British advanced on Washington D.C. Nothing stood in their way, since the American forces had fled before the much-stronger British forces. Washington D.C was put to the torch! Fortunately though, the wife of President James Madison, Dolly Madison, saved many White House art treasures before she, her husband, and the rest of the government officials fled the city! Yet the British forces and their destruction of the city came to an abrupt halt courtesy of a rare hurricane, followed by an even rarer tornado! The British troops were decimated! A fiction writer would lose all credibility if he/she made this stuff up!

The year of 1814 is notable for another War Of 1812 episode. From aboard a ship in the harbor, a certain Francis Scott Key watched as British forces bombarded U.S. defenses at Fort McHenry in Baltimore. The shelling continued all through the night, yet the next morning, Scott Key saw that the American flag still flew over the fort! Inspired by the glorious sight, Francis Scott Key penned the lyrics to a little song called, "The Star Spangled Banner!"

Historically speaking, the year 1820 is nothing to sneeze at either. True, that particular date in U.S. history doesn't have the eye-catching headlines of the sort you saw in 1814. Still, it was the year that King George III of England (certainly a pivotal figure in American history) died. It was also in 1820 that the "Missouri Compromise" legislation prohibited slavery above a certain latitude and longitude in the United States. A result of the Missouri Compromise was that Maine entered the Union as a free state, while Missouri entered as a slave state in 1821. Also in 1820, the American Colonization Society sent 88 free blacks to settle Liberia in Africa.

Ok, in terms of historical value, it's my opinion that an 1814 dime beats an 1820 dime. Now let's discuss the afore-mentioned scarcity/value ratio. As far as scarcity, we already know the 1814 Capped Bust dime is harder to find than the 1820– in fact, the mintage of the 1814 dime is less than half that of the 1820 dime. Yet, as of this writing, the value of the 1814 dime in Good condition is $30, while the value of an 1820 dime in the same condition is $25. In Very Good condition, the 1814 dime is valued at only $40 while the 1820 dime is valued at $35. That's just a $5 difference! Clearly, the 1814 Bust dime HAS to be the better value. But even that little mintage/value comparison doesn't tell the whole story.

The mintage for the 1814 Capped Bust dime may be a good deal lower than that of the 1820 Capped Bust dime, still, there were some 421,000 1814 dimes struck. That shouldn't make it a particularly rare coin. Relatively scarce, perhaps. From my observations, however, the 1814 Bust dime seems to be a good deal harder to find than even its mintage of just under half a million would indicate. Do the eBay test. Do a search on 1820 Bust dimes. You should find at least a small selection of them up for bid. But some weeks, not a single 1814 Bust dime is listed! Not even the quite scarce and sought-after 1793 U.S. Chain cent can make THAT claim! In short, it would seem that the 1820 Bust dime is a bit overvalued. Or the 1814 Bust dime is blatantly UNDER-valued. I believe it's the latter.

If your budget won't allow you to go after the 1794-1807 U.S. silver coins, why not go after the 1814 Capped Bust dime? Unlike, say, the 1814 Capped Bust half dollar, the 1814 Bust dime was a work-horse coin of the populace, far more likely to be passed hand-to-hand as small change than to be saved as a high-denomination coin. Not only that, the 1814 dime was struck during a perilous time in our nation's history: the years of the War Of 1812. The 1814 Capped Bust dime is a good deal harder to track down than other Capped Bust dime dates, but it's hardly valued higher than other, more common dates! However, if your search for an 1814 Bust dime proves fruitless, an 1820 date is a pretty good affordable alternate "Early U.S." silver coin.

CHAPTER THIRTY-SEVEN

THE IDENTITY OF AMERICA'S FIRST COIN – REVEALED!

L adies and Gentlemen, we have a winner. Up until now, we've discussed a number of coins that are either strong candidates for the title of "America's First Coin," or are a "first" coin of some sense in the pantheon of early United States coins. But now I'm prepared to raise the arm of a victor and bestow upon that victor the title of "America's First Coin." As the winner, this coin deserves a hallowed spot in all U.S. coin guide books that discuss Colonial coins. This coin begat not just 400 years of circulating coin in the United States, but arguably, paper money as well — any kind of hard money with inscribed images and legends stating the authority under which that hard money circulates. From this humble coin sprang America's shops, businesses, real estate transactions, homes, banks, churches, stock markets! Yes, I have chosen a winner. Furthermore, I will spend the duration of this chapter defending my choice.

And how will I defend my choice? In two simple words: Edward Hayes. Ever heard of him? Probably not. There was never a movie or major book about his life. In fact, Edward

Hayes is rarely even mentioned in history books, even those written about the period in which he lived! But Edward Hayes is crucial to THIS book. Edward Hayes has everything to do with my choice for "America's First Coin." That said, I should warn you — you might want to avoid driving or operating heavy machinery while reading the paragraphs that follow. It's not exactly riveting stuff, but stick with me on this.

First the basics. Edward Hayes was a citizen of England. His life began around 1550 and ended around 1620. Those dates aren't too important — what *is* important to know is that his prime adult years spanned from the Tudor Age of Elizabeth I through the Stuart Age of James I. As far as is known, he never lived in America. But for years, he seems to have been virtually obsessed with the notion of British colonization in the New World.

What kind of man was Edward Hayes? I think I can paint a pretty good picture of him if you can imagine the following scenario: the CEO of Universal Studios is seated at the head of the table in the Universal Studios Board Room. Also seated at the table is his top assistant, as well as the other Universal Studios executives.

"Who are we seeing today?" asks Mr. CEO of his assistant.

"Edward Hayes is first on the list," answers the assistant. There are knowing chuckles. A couple of executives roll their eyes.

"Again?" asks Mr. CEO, incredulously.

"Afraid so," answers the assistant, "But Mr. Hayes says this idea is REALLY big."

"He always says that," sighs Mr. CEO, "Tell me again why we listen to his pitches so much?"

"Well," answers the assistant, "he's been in the business a number of years, and he's helped get some major film projects off the ground."

"All right, show him in," says Mr. CEO, a hint of resignation in his voice.

The boardroom door opens, and in marches an eager-looking Edward Hayes. He stands before the boardroom table, facing the CEO of Universal Studios. Without a moment's hesitation, Edward Hayes gets right to it:

"Ok, picture this: Superman versus Batman in a 3-D Battle Royal.....!"

Hopefully you get the picture. No, Edward Hayes wasn't in show business. But he was a man with big ideas. Not that he was a Ralph Kramden type, an epic dreamer but a highly unsuccessful doer. Edward Hayes was very much a "doer," even if he is not remembered for being an adventurer on the level of, say, Sir Francis Drake. In his work, Edward Hayes: Liverpool Colonial Pioneer, historian David B. Quinn writes:

> *Edward Hayes was, first and foremost, a projector.*
> *The main, abiding interest of his life was in thinking*
> *up speculative schemes of one sort or another and,*
> *usually, putting them before government officials...*
> *Should one of them be taken up he might get rewards*
> *in the shape of office or even power.*

In addition to being a lifelong "schemer" and "projector,"Edward Hayes was also an accomplished seaman and voyager. In 1583, his ship, the *Golden Hind*, was the only one of five vessels to return back to England after exploring the coasts of Newfoundland and what is today, New England. From this voyage, Captain Edward Hayes apparently became enamored with the idea of England colonizing the New World. In fact, for the remainder of the 1580's, Hayes campaigned or "projected" vigorously for an establishment of an English fishery and settlement in Newfoundland. For a time, Hayes equally promoted the idea of a similar fishery and settlement in what is today, the New England coast of the United States. But the idea of English control of "Norumbega," (as the New England coast was known in the 1580's) was abandoned in order to focus his energies more on the English settlement of Newfoundland.

Still with me? We're getting closer to the point, believe me. The long and short of it is, Hayes' dream of a British Newfoundland fishery and settlement did not come to pass. But Hayes never lost his interest in promoting New World settlement to the crown and to the movers and shakers of Britain. Edward Hayes turns up in the pages of history a few years later — this time enthusiastically promoting his idea for financing the Virginia Company. Of course, if you know your history, then you know it was the Virginia Company that sponsored and sent settlers to Virginia in the New World, resulting in a settlement that would become Jamestown. Though not proven, it is speculated that Edward Hayes was in close contact with Sir Thomas Smyth, leader of the "southerners," the Virginia Company settlers who would settle in the Chesapeake Bay area of Virginia (as opposed to the "northerners" who would settle in the New England area of Virginia), as Hayes had been living at the house of Smyth's sister, Lady Scott. In any event, Hayes' idea for the Virginia Company was to get Parliament involved in the enterprise, but this idea didn't take. All this is to say that Edward Hayes seems to have been a prominent voice during the formation of the Virginia Company. Did Edward Hayes ever set foot in Jamestown? Not that we know of, but if he did, it was as a visitor, not as a settler.

In summing up the little-known legacy of Edward Hayes, David B. Quinn writes:

> *If we look back over his career it is evident that Edward Hayes occupies a position of some significance in the early colonizing movement. He was*

actively concerned with North America.. From the grant of a colonizing patent to Sir Humphrey Gilbert in 1578 down to the issue of the Virginia Company Charter in 1607... Hayes took a longer continuous part in the debate [of English colonization in the New World] *than anyone else except Richard Hakluyt..."*

Our story of Edward Hayes would seem to end there, were it not for one of Edward Hayes' OTHER promotional ventures. In addition to his ambitious "pitches" (to use a Hollywood term) for English settlements and business enterprises in the New World, Hayes found the time to promote a different venture altogether: coinage.

"Picture this," says an enthusiastic Captain Edward Hayes as he stands before a prominent official of the court of Queen Elizabeth I, "A new kind of coin for the man of humble means! A coin of humble value — but instead of striking teeny-tiny silver coins, how about an official COPPER coin of the realm!"

Ok, I took creative license with setting up the dialogue in the aforementioned scene, but the point is, from 1579 to 1613, Edward Hayes tirelessly pushed his idea for a royally authorized copper coin of England. At this time, during the reign of Elizabeth I, there were tiny silver coins of halfpenny and three-farthing denominations, but no base-metal coinage for even smaller transactions. Consequently, numerous privately and crudely struck lead tokens served as a kind of coinage for the common man of England. No doubt, Hayes saw the need for copper coinage, and doubtlessly saw an opportunity for profit, both for the crown, and for himself.

England never adopted Hayes' idea for an official copper coinage — not during his lifetime anyway, though King James I did at last authorize privately-contracted patent copper farthings in 1613. Still, Hayes was not just a proponent of tinkering with the coinage of England — he had ideas for the coinage of Ireland as well. For instance, in 1602, Edward Hayes proposed debased silver shillings for Ireland, shillings that would be valued at ninepence in England. But more importantly — and now is the time to pay attention – in 1601, Hayes' idea for a copper coinage at last came to fruition. A copper coinage, not for England, but struck in England for use in Ireland. These were the copper halfpenny and penny tokens, struck for use in Ireland in the years 1601 and 1602. Two dozen of these Irish copper tokens were excavated in recent years at the Jamestown Fort site in Virginia!

So there you have it. Edward Hayes: New World promoter, Virginia Company enthusiast, and at the very least, the unofficial catalyst behind the 1601-02 Irish copper tokens — the ONLY coin type excavated in any kind of quantity at the site of our nation's first permanent settlement, Jamestown! From what we know of his strong desire to promote his new ventures, would it be a safe guess that Edward Hayes had something to do with the small supply of Irish copper tokens that have turned up at the 1607-10 Jamestown Fort site? Does the trail of "first coin" originator lead back to one man: a certain, Edward Hayes? I don't know how many lawyers would agree with me, but preponderance of the evidence compels me to pronounce Edward Hayes of Liverpool, England... GUILTY!

CONCLUSION

Though I have listed prices one can expect to pay for the coins described in this book, I hope you, the reader, will not become too focused on the prices quoted. From my own experience, books on coin collecting (and I'm not talking just about price guides) that place a strong emphasis on listing retail prices, do not age well. Such books seemed to proliferate in the U.S. back in the 1950's and 1960's. There was a coin-collecting boom at the time, and everybody was looking through their piggy-banks and pocket change for scarce-date Lincoln cents or Jefferson nickels. As a result, books meant to introduce beginners to coin collecting were price-guide heavy. Your local library may well still carry such books. Think you can even begin to trust the retail prices listed in those books today? Hardly.

My point is, retail prices may go up or down, or may even stay the same over a period of years. Relative affordability and availability are more stable factors. That's a fancy way of saying that a commonly available coin today, will likely be commonly available in the future. Likewise, a coin that's hard-to-find now will not likely be any easier to find in the future. A coin that doesn't cost a lot now will probably not cost a lot (in relation to current incomes) in the future. A coin that is costly now will still be costly in the future. Are there exceptions to this rule? Of course!

But isn't it possible for a coin to quickly rise in value? Absolutely. That's been proven time and time again. For that to happen, however, there must be a sharp upswing in demand for that particular coin. Heavy demand drives up the value of coins that are scarce or even not-so-scarce. The difference is, values REALLY shoot up when suddenly there is strong demand for a coin that was scarce to begin with! Remember, a genuinely scarce coin may only be worth a few dollars if there are even fewer collectors around who want that coin!

What's an example of a common coin that has soared in value? How about any Morgan silver dollar of 1878-1921 in early 1980? At the time, an investment firm was trying to corner the market on silver. Common wisdom said silver was going to become very scarce very quickly. Everybody – the average man on the street and coin dealers alike — rushed out to buy (and sell) silver. Silver prices rose to nearly $50 an ounce! Common silver dollars skyrocketed in value. Then the silver market crashed. The prices for common-date Morgan silver dollars plummeted.

Let's get back to the coins featured in this book. Any chance there will be a sharp spike in demand for these coins? Well, I can say this — I shudder to think how much you would have to pay, and how hard you would have to look, if as many collectors go after these coins as go after, say, Lincoln cents! Nearly every coin or token I've listed is what I would classify as "scarce, but available." These pieces are not terribly hard-to-find simply because rabid hordes of collectors and investors are NOT chasing after them! Forget a huge influx of new collectors – if even half the population of CURRENT coin collectors suddenly had to have these coins, they would vanish from dealer inventories. Quickly. The ones left on the market would almost certainly carry a high price tag.

Could not such a scenario happen, especially since I'm blabbing to the world about how important these historical coins are? Oh.. maybe. That is, if enough people suddenly become enlightened as to the importance of these pieces courtesy of this book (a very flattering thought) or simply educate themselves about these treasures from other sources. Still, though it would be great to think this humble little book has the potential to rock the numismatic world, I somehow don't envision a mad collector rush to buy Nuremberg jettons or William III halfpennies. Think Lincoln cents. Think Morgan dollars. Think PCGS. Think MS-69.

I can see your reaction now: "Huh?" So a little clarification is in order.

With any luck, you've been inspired by the history and stories behind the pieces you've read about in the previous chapters. Perhaps you now have the urge to go out and find one of these historical treasures. It won't matter to you if the coins are worn, or even a little damaged, just as long as you can tell what it is. The important thing is the STORY your much-handled coin has to tell! If that's the case, then you're a lot like me in that respect. But you/we actually represent only a small segment of the coin collecting universe!

Even if this book makes the New York Times bestseller list, a lot more collectors (especially in the United States) will want to complete a date and mintmark set of Lincoln cents than will want to obtain James I farthings! I also believe that a big, shiny, Morgan silver dollar dated in the 1880's will hold more fascination to more coin collectors than will a well-worn French copper coin of the 1650's — even if that same copper coin might have circulated in Colonial America!

I should be clear on this — there is NOTHING wrong with any collector preferring Lincoln cents or Morgan dollars to James I farthings or William III halfpennies. Let's face it, it's much easier for a citizen of our country to understand and appreciate older products of the U.S. Mint than some REALLY old, worn, European copper coin with legends in Latin, and designs featuring a shield of arms or some Old

World monarch. And what did I mean by "Think PCGS" and "Think MS-69?" Well, PCGS stands for *Professional Coin Grading Services*. MS-69 (Mint-State-69) is a grade given to a coin in virtually flawless uncirculated condition, there being an eleven-point scale of "uncirculated," (MS-60 to MS-70). I bring up both of these terms to represent the very huge segment of the coin collecting community that considers "grade" to be all-important. These are collectors who won't settle for any coin of inferior quality, rare, historical, or otherwise. These collectors, while they love the coins they obtain, usually maintain a strong eye towards their coin's future investment potential. And what coins are most likely to bring a strong return as an investment? Oh, a coin that's, say, MS-65 or higher. And who determines whether a coin is MS-63 or MS-65 or even MS-70? That would be PCGS or another of the highly regarded professional grading services out there. The grade these professional graders bestow upon a coin can officially mean the difference between a value of, say, $200 or $2,000!

Again, let's be clear. The collector who purchases only flawless 20th century United States coins graded by a professional grading service is not likely to compete with you for a heavily-thumbed 1775 Spanish two reales with a rim bump or two. That is not to put down his or her collecting choice. Some collect coins for investment. Some collect coins for artistic beauty. Some collect only one type of coin because they happen to like a particular coin series. There is no right or wrong in what one chooses to collect. My point is that with the variety of collecting tastes out there, AND with the proven heavy interest in 19th to 21st century U.S. coins, there's not likely to be a mass rush for the relatively obscure coins and tokens we've talked about here.

In closing, I'll reference a scene from the classic 1981 thriller, *Raiders Of The Lost Ark*. In the movie, our hero, Indiana Jones, confronts the evil French archaeologist who not only has taken possession of the Ark of The Covenant, but Indiana's sweetheart as well! Indiana aims his bazooka at the Ark and declares that he will blow up the ancient relic if the woman is not released. The evil French archaeologist merely smiles and reminds Indiana that they are two of a kind, men who have dedicated their lives to seeking out and preserving historical treasures.

Then, the Frenchman pats the Ark and says to Indiana, "You and I, we're just passing through history. THIS, Indiana Jones... this IS history." With that, the villainous relic-digger steps aside and invites Indiana to blow up the priceless treasure. Indiana cannot.

I always liked that little speech, even though it came from the lips of a weasel. Coin collectors can say the same thing about THEIR treasures! So go out, find some of the coins and tokens you've read about here, and plunk down a few dollars for them. It will be money well spent. Then, you can tell anyone who will listen, "You and I are just passing through history. This coin IS history!"

BIBLIOGRAPHY/SELECTED READING:

Anton Jr., William T.; Kesse, Bruce <u>Forgotten Coins of the North American Colonies</u> Krause Publications, Iola, WI 1992

Hume, Ivor Noel. <u>The Virginia Adventure (Roanoke To Jamestown, An Archaeological andHistorical Odyssey</u>) Alfred A. Knopf, New York 1994, pp. 37-39

Hume, Ivor Noel. <u>Martin's Hundred</u> Alfred A. Knopf, New York 1982, pp. 17-19, 189, 224-26, 317-18

Kelso, William M. <u>Jamestown Rediscovery I: Search For 1607 James Fort</u> Association for the Preservation of Virginia Antiquities, 1995 pp. 14-16

Lasser, Joseph R. <u>The Coins Of Colonial America: World Trade Coins of the Seventeenth and Eighteenth Centuries</u> The Colonial Williamsburg Foundation, 1997

Quinn, David B. <u>North America From Earliest Discovery</u> Harper & Row, New York 1973 pp. 324-25, 364, 388-93, 419-23

Quinn, David B. Edward Hayes: Liverpool Colonial Pioneer Reprinted from the Transactions Of The Historic Society Of Lancashire And Cheshire, Vol. III 1959 pp. 25-45

Reinstedt, Randall A. Tales, Treasures and Pirates of Old Monterey Ghost Town Publications, Carmel, CA 1976 pp.53-60

magazine articles:

Gibbs, William T. "First European colony site in America's yields coinage" *Coin World* magazine, February 26, 1996 pg. 75

Giedroye, Richard. "Collectors help identify Independence Hall find" *Coin World* magazine, September 23, 1996 pg. 3

Iddings, John. "The John J. Ford Collection" *COINage* magazine, August 2003

websites:

APVA Preservation Virginia. http//www.apva.org

The California State Military Museum www.militarymuseum.org/Expeditions.html California State Military Department

The Coins of Colonial and Early America. http//www.coins.nd.edu/ColCoin/

A Project of the Robert H. Gore, Jr. Numismatic Endowment University of Norte Dame, <u>Department of Special Collections</u> by Louis Jordan

CPSIA information can be obtained at www.ICGtesting.com
Printed in the USA
LVOW12s1700040414

380383LV00001B/176/A